ECOVILLAGE

1001 ways to heal the planet

For Shelley,

With love, respect and joy —

Thank you!

Kosha

Edited by: Kosha Joubert and Leila Dregger

Published by:
Triarchy Press
Station Offices
Axminster
Devon
EX13 5PF
United Kingdom
+44 (0)1297 631456

info@triarchypress.net
www.triarchypress.net

A catalogue record for this book is available from the British Library.

Print ISBN: 978-1-909470-75-0

Cover

The photo is entitled *Curious Girl in the Peace Community, San José de Apartado in Columbia* and was taken by Ludwig Schramm.

Contents

EUROPE

AFRICA

Photo: Torre Superiore

Appreciation

This book was born from a rich mix of minds and places. Our first priority is to thank our storytellers who have so generously contributed to life in the ecovillages and to this book in particular. We give thanks to all the elders of the ecovillage networks who had the wisdom to plant seeds and watch them grow, and especially to Hildur and Ross Jackson and the Gaia Trust. We give thanks to the vibrant young people, who have the vision and enthusiasm to bring the movement into the next level of aliveness and readiness. We give thanks to all those who are doing the actual work on the ground right now. After reading this book we all know intimately just how much continuous courage, perseverance and caring it takes!

Special thanks go to our voluntary translators, photographers, editors and researchers amongst them Jenefer Marquis, Angelika Gander, Pavitra Mueller and Ethan Hirsch-Tauber. Clio Pauly from Namibia was our star and a never-ending source of clarity and commitment to seeing details through to the end. Huge thanks to the great publishing team at Triarchy Press for your encouragement and support! We warmly appreciate our family and friends, and our communities at Findhorn and Tamera for holding and inspiring us...

And lastly, a heartfelt thank you goes out to you, the reader, for going on this adventurous journey with us! We look forward to our paths crossing in the future.

ECOVILLAGES *are intentional or traditional communities that aim to regenerate social and natural environments. The social, ecological, economic and cultural dimensions of sustainability are integrated into a holistic sustainable development model that is adapted to local contexts.*

Ecovillages are consciously designed through locally owned participatory processes.

In this book we also include networks of ecovillages and NGOs that support communities to design their own pathway into the future and to transition to being ecovillages.

Preface

All over the planet, and often in unseen, remote places, one of the most crucial explorations of humankind is in full swing. Scientists and technicians, inventors and farmers, women and men with huge hearts and youth with fresh eyes, activists and those most affected by the global crises are building a network of integrity together: in villages, cities and slums, they are finding answers to the questions of our times, stepping into response-ability and initiating ways of living that sustain life and regenerate our social and natural systems. No one planned this community-led movement of meaningful response; instead, it emerged from the hearts, minds and hands of courageous people who decided to choose the road less travelled.

> 'Two roads diverged in a yellow wood... I took the one less
> travelled by, And that has made all the difference.'
> Robert Frost

While in so many places 'business as usual' continues as if we were blissfully unaware of the consequences, ecovillages work to implement solutions on the ground — mostly with simple means, but sometimes with spectacular results. They have become regional and national beacons of inspiration for the social, cultural, ecological and economic revival of rural and urban areas. They are part of a worldwide movement for social and environmental justice.

When the concept of ecovillages first arose in the late 1980s, it related to intentional communities, born from the dedication to create high quality, low impact lifestyles that offer an alternative to a culture of consumerism and exploitation. Today, and especially in the Global South, the ecovillage networks include thousands of traditional villages and initiatives in slums where people have decided to take their future into their own hands. Growing from a shared set of values, the flow of communication between ecovillages from all continents facilitates North-South reconciliation, East-West dialogues and, in effect, an evolving global consciousness.

In this book you will be introduced to a selection of ecovillage projects from all over the world. We have aimed to give at least a taste of their richness and diversity. Most texts are based on interviews with founders or long-standing members of communities; some texts are about regional or national networks of ecovillage transition. As we celebrate the 20th anniversary of the Global Ecovillage Network in 2015, we want to honour successes, but also learn from difficulties and failure. Consequently, this book, while outlining one of the greatest adventures of our time, our quest for lifestyles of sustainability, does so from a very personal point of view.

At the end of each article, you will find a few keywords for solutions. Every ecovillage is developing local solutions to global challenges. You are invited to find out more about some of these solutions in the Solution Library (*solution.ecovillage.org*) where they are made accessible to all. You might even feel inspired to integrate some of them in your own community or back garden.

This book is simultaneously being published in German by the publishing house 'Neue Erde', in a version that is more focused on examples from the German-speaking world.

May the stories and tales come as a source of inspiration to all of us. May they strengthen our belief in our capacity to realise our dreams and become true care-takers of our beautiful planet and each other. We are all needed in this quest — every single one of us is called to take a next step on our own version of the road less travelled by. Maybe, one day, these roads will merge into a new, life-sustaining culture.

Enjoy!
Kosha Joubert
Leila Dregger

Please note: Unless otherwise shown, all photographs come from the ecovillage featured.

spotlights within a global movement
Did you know...?

...that the first ecovillage in the Democratic Republic of Congo will be in Buhama, and will be built by and for the Pygmies?

...that the ecovillage Crystal Waters in Australia, with a population of over 200, simultaneously acts as a wildlife reserve?

...that in Oriya, India, GEN has been reaching out to a network of 4,000 tribal villages, many of whom are recognised now as ecovillages?

...that for 13 years in Latin America, the travelling community of La Caravana taught thouands of villagers, farmers, youth and children sustainable techniques?

...that the gASTWERKe Community in Germany uses alternative economics, consensus decision-making and conscious consumption, and also requires pro-active involvement in social and political conflicts?

...that the ecovillage Hurdal in Norway developed the Active House? It has made a green business of building eco-friendly houses.

...that Eco-Valley in Hungary produces enough grain and vegetables to feed its 200 residents, and offers social work to poor communities nationwide?

...that the ecovillage Twin Oaks in Virginia, USA has already existed for nearly 50 years and relies on the production of tofu, hanging mats and solar energy?

...that the Konohana Family, based at the foot of Mt. Fuji in Japan, has around 100 members who are engaged in new agricultural methods for healthy food production. It is also connected to the care of psychiatrically unwell people.

...that La Cité Ecologique in Quebec, Canada, started as an alternative school and today successfully combines green business and nature conservation?

...that Dancing Rabbit ecovillage in northeastern Missouri is creating a model for ecological and social sustainability to demonstrate to US society what a high quality, low resource consumption lifestyle can look like?

...that the ecovillage Schloss Tempelhof in Germany, with its economic and legal know-how, is supporting many other ecovillages and communities as they emerge?

Ecovillages and the Beautiful World We Could Live In
by Kosha Joubert

"We are the last generation that can change climate change. We have a duty to act." Ban Ki-moon

This is a beautiful planet! It calls to us to take time to explore - to visit a river, look at the moon, watch the wind as it moves through the leaves, listen to birdsong, feel the ocean waters on our skin – to allow ourselves to be touched by the larger forces that surround us. And we only need to look into the eyes of a child to connect to our innate wish to protect life. I believe we carry a natural tendency to care, and feel happiest when we find a way to express it.[1]

While this may be true, many of us live lifestyles that keep us glued to electronic screens, confined in built-up environments and surrounded by consumer products. As we witness the convergence of multiple crises resulting from our mainstream actions and institutions (climate change, ecocide, poverty, senseless violence, the depletion of natural resources, pollution, etc.) many of us long to shift to a lifestyle that enables us to tread softly on this earth. We long to marry passion with responsibility and our love for the planet with the ability to earn a living. We long to one day look back and feel proud of the heritage we've left our children and grandchildren.

The ecovillage networks that span the planet are a tangible expression of these longings.

I was born in 1968, in South Africa, a country where people of different skin colours were separated by force under the system of apartheid. Economic exploitation, land grabbing, humiliation, pain, threat and fear were normal occurrences under apartheid. The consequences of this brutal system are still playing out in South African society today; for example, it is estimated that a woman is raped every 36 seconds[2]. It is not a simple feat to heal the individual and collective scars of trauma and historic atrocities. Forgiveness and reconciliation cannot be legislated for; they need to be lived, like a road that needs to be walked through time.

Coming from this background, my focus has been firmly lodged in spaces of healing and transition, and in fields of intercultural communication. I developed a healthy mistrust of political institutions, closed systems and societal norms. What seems more trustworthy, instead, is searching the edge, coming down to the ground, meeting the people, welcoming tangible experience and the general messiness and complexity

---

1 www.theguardian.com/lifeandstyle/2014/nov/03/ten-easy-steps-that-will-make-you-a-happier-person
2 http://africacheck.org/reports/will-74400-women-be-raped-this-august-in-south-africa/

of life. My engagement with the ecovillage and intentional community movement has been inspired by all the above.

When I turned 23, I went on a pilgrimage through my home country at a time when violence was at its peak. It was in 1991 and Nelson Mandela had just been released. The country was bristling with suppressed anger and frustrated hope. For a while, I had worked for various anti-apartheid organisations. Now, at last, I had the courage to walk an actual exploration of my country, to visit all those places that were taboo to a young white 'Afrikanermeisie': the black taxis, the townships, wilderness and night sky-solitude. I walked up the coast for three months, ending up in the Transkei, one of the black homelands at that time.

Once I had crossed the river by boat at Port St. Johns, there were only footpaths, meandering around hills, over brooks, to huts and fields that perfectly blended in with the landscape. The horns of African cattle curved like everything else here, and their pride and curiosity spoke of partnership rather than of subjugation by their human owners. In this place of beauty, I found a community where black and white young people were living together, fleeing the system of apartheid and tilling the soil, taking care of the land, building huts and bringing up their children in unison.

This was my first experience of an 'ecovillage', even though none of us knew the term at that time. It changed my life. I realised that we could build the new within the old without fighting. I understood that such a 'cell' or niche of innovation could inspire a movement of change throughout a whole system. I also realised that the luxurious simplicity of living in accordance with one's values requires a process of inner growth and maturation that mercilessly chisels away at naivety, innocence and false pretence!

I had discovered an entrance to a new world, hidden like an onion skin within the one I was introduced to by mainstream education: the world of intentional communities and ecovillages. When I arrived in Europe and later travelled to Asia, I followed word of mouth recommendations like a red thread and was guided from one magical place to the next. Each place was different, born from a specific intention within a particular cultural context, yet all were similar in their search for a life that could become an expression of love.

The Global Ecovillage Network (GEN) was founded in 1995 to make visible an emergence that was already taking place, and to provide a link between communities being developed by thousands of grassroots pioneers. GEN serves as an alliance between rural and urban, traditional and intentional communities aiming for high-quality, low-impact lifestyles. GEN has settlements with some of the lowest recorded per capita carbon footprints.

GEN works through five regional organisations: the Ecovillage Networks of North America (ENA), Latin America (El Consejo de Asentamientos Sustentables de las Américas / CASA), Oceania and Asia (GENOA), Europe and the Middle East (GEN-Europe), and of Africa (GEN-Africa). NextGEN brings together the youth movement. Together these networks connect to the impressive work done in over 10,000 communities on the ground in more than 100 countries worldwide. Weaving together the most innovative solutions with deep-rooted traditional knowledge, GEN is creating a font of wisdom for sustainable living on a global scale.

From permaculture projects in Africa to Buddhist ashrams in Asia, from hippie communes in the USA to eco-caravans in Latin America, there is a burgeoning diversity of 'ecovillage projects'. The sheer complexity and range of expression seem to be at the core of what 'ecovillage' is all about! Our human and natural diversity is precious and lies at the core of our hope for resilience. The wealth of variety is one of our greatest treasures and may manifest in the artistic nature of individual expression, the richness of spiritual diversity, and the ingenuity of locally appropriate technologies.

Within this celebration of difference there is a common core and GEN defines ecovillages as intentional or traditional communities, consciously designed through locally owned, participatory processes to regenerate social and natural environments. The four dimensions of sustainability (ecology, economy, the social and cultural) are integrated into a holistic, sustainable development model that is adapted to local requirements.

Ecovillages combine a supportive and high-quality social and cultural environment with a low-impact way of life. They are precious playgrounds in which groups of committed people can experiment to find solutions for some of the challenges we face globally. Rapidly gaining recognition as demonstration sites of sustainability in practice, ecovillages naturally become places of inspiration within their regions and societies. Within them, new approaches can be seen, tasted and touched.

Ideally, every village and every city on this planet would become an ecovillage or a green city, with eco-neigbourhoods. We seem to think that we cannot live on this earth without destroying the very foundations that our life rests upon. But ecovillages showcase what old wisdom traditions taught: that communities can both sustain and regenerate life through intelligent and loving interventions. In community, we can replenish soils, diversify ecosystems, replant forests and purify waters; we can heal wounds of the past; find solutions; we can live in a web of fulfilling human relationships. All the necessary ingredients are available, if we would only dedicate our hearts and our minds to this most crucial endeavour: the transition to a viable future.

A core question arises: how can the ecovillage approach be disseminated at scale without losing its core values? One of the answers comes with education. At GEN's 10th anniversary celebration in 2005, Gaia Education

19

was launched as its educational arm to bring the learning from ecovillages to the broader public.

I was deeply honoured to be amongst 24 ecovillage educators from around the world who met in Findhorn, Scotland, in 2004, to bring together the best of what we wanted to share. The Ecovillage Design Education Curriculum (EDE) was born and became a recognised contribution to the UN Decade of Education for Sustainable Development, 2004-2014. The EDE is a 4-week long training, universal in scope but local in application. Through the EDE, communities can design their own pathways into the future, combining existing strengths in all four dimensions of sustainability with leverage points for successful change. Today, the EDE has been delivered in 34 countries around the world, and is being developed into Bachelor and Masters degree courses.

A second answer lies in closer collaboration with other sectors of society. During the first years of GEN, ecovillages tended to act as islands turning inwards on themselves. Today ecovillages are opening up, and seeing themselves as an integral part of a much broader movement of change. GEN is building alliances, not only with like-minded organisations such as Transition Town and Permaculture Networks, but also with governmental authorities, corporations and academia.

We can also learn from current examples in Senegal and Thailand, where bridges between civil society, governmental decision-makers and the corporate sector are supporting community-led responses to climate change on regional and national levels. GEN-Senegal was formed in 2002, showcasing best practices like solar cookers, drip irrigation, permaculture design and reforestation programmes in a network of 45 ecovillages. The Senegalese government, inspired by these examples, later established a National Agency for Ecovillages, ANEV, positioned within the Ministry of Environment and Sustainable Development. Today, Senegal is the first country in the world to create an integrated national ecovillage programme, dedicated to transitioning 14,000 traditional villages to ecovillages[3]. In December 2014, a Global Ecovillage Summit was hosted by GEN in collaboration with the Senegalese Government. The Senegalese Prime Minister, addressing the ecovillage delegates from 40 countries, expressed his personal commitment, as well as that of his President, to promote the ecovillage concept across the African continent.

GEN and the EDE provide invaluable ways of reaching beyond hopeful visions and mere words to true community empowerment. Local communities become inspired to design their own pathways into the future and start influencing decision-makers and policies through an 'Adaptive Governance Cycle ' that marries bottom-up with top-down approaches. It

20

3 www.africanouvelles.com/nouvelles/afrique/5115-senegal-14-000-ecovillages-seront-crees-dici-2020.html

brings people a step closer to a true democracy that trusts in the inherent wisdom of people.

One of the most underutilised resources we have on the planet today is the good intentions of citizens and our willingness to make a difference. GEN helps to unleash this potential and provides a glimpse into the beautiful world that can emerge from many thousands of local solutions, woven into one colourful tapestry of resilience. This is the time to heal apartheid, not on the level of any one country, but within humanity as a whole. Within the networks of GEN, when Boniface from Bangladesh, Lua from DRCongo, Margarita from Colombia, Claudian from Romania and Aida from Palestine gather to share what is happening in their communities, we move beyond any concept of global awareness and go straight to the heart of humanity. We know that we are one, celebrating our successes and mourning our losses together. We are all on the same journey – answering the call of future generations to wake up.

> *"Another world is not only possible, she is on her way. On a quiet day, I can hear her breathing."* Arundhati Roy

21

The Power of Community
by Leila Dregger

Core Competencies of Ecovillages

In the Occupy movement over the past few years, whether on Wall Street, in Madrid or in Cairo, one phenomenon has kept cropping up: young people — today, so often primed for competition and pressured to perform, but sobered by the lack of meaningful prospects — experienced the miracle of community. Again and again, realising that their problems were shared by others, they joined forces and together found out-of-the-box solutions. They invented new forms of communication and democratic rules, shared their food and their thoughts, came up with collective action, experienced love and felt understood. Anything seemed possible! Hardly anyone wanted to go back home. This was real life and they never wanted it to stop.

They had found gold dust — but after a short while it began to run through their fingers. As endless discussions dealt with banalities and the essential issues were no longer addressed; as the majority fell silent and the rest argued endlessly — the exhausting hamster wheel of competition began to turn again. There was a lack of experience and knowledge about how to unite a group more permanently. The dream shattered — often some time before the police and the army cleared the camps.

This is not surprising. The dominant paradigm in today´s society is still: 'best to trust yourself'. In politics, business and everyday life we are still used to competition, separation and working against one another, and this stance also dominates our emotional inner world.

This is how most of us were conditioned — and this is how we will drive the Earth to its ruin. Without the authentic experience of wholeness and community, without feeling what connects us and without this "web of kinship, the invisible glue that binds us" (Albert Bates), we will not be able to react jointly, quickly and effectively to a world that is changing faster and faster.

On closer analysis it seems that most of the innovative projects and initiatives that fail do not do so because of external threats, but because of internal quarrels — power struggles, secrecy or jealousy. Imagine how climate negotiations would develop if politicians and lobbyists were to detach themselves from their own individual interests and work resolutely for the common good. In order for the 'beautiful world' that we dream about to become reality, we need to create a new social paradigm with communities of trust at its core.

This is precisely the core competence that ecovillages and intentional communities bring to the table. For all their diversity, they have one thing in common: they have decided to deal with their issues and challenges as a community — and to continue doing so in spite of the conflicts, difficulties and signs of fatigue that inevitably occur. Those communities that have survived their ups and downs, their experiments and mistakes, that have risen from the ashes again and again and that continue to exist, often into the second or third generation, have collected valuable experiences and are willing to pass them on.

What is community?

Everything lives in community. From planetary systems to groups of cells, all life finds its place and its uniqueness through interactions with others, within the framework of a greater whole. As single-celled organisms became multi-cellular, the possibilities of perception and movement multiplied. In a healthy organism, each organ relies on the other. No liver has to fight a kidney for oxygen. No lung ever thinks that it needs to act just like the heart. It is only together, in their diversity, coordinated through the mysterious principle of self-organisation — our great evolutionary ally — that they are successful. The biologist Bruce Lipton says: "If the cells in a body were living in competition and distrust, the way humans do among each other, they would fall apart almost immediately."

The community is the original home of humans. As the archaeologist Marija Gimbutas and many other historians describe it, the original tribal cultures that existed worldwide knew relatively little violence or punishment. Sexuality, she maintains, was often dealt with in a relaxed way, women and men were relatively equal and instead of a hierarchy there was probably a circle in which decisions were taken together. Judging by the millennia that these cultures existed, they must have lived sustainably. If the life of an animal or a plant had to be taken, it seems to have been done with respect. Tribes sensed when they had reached an ecological limit and moved on. In this context, enriching oneself at the expense of the community was not simply a sign of immorality, but of insanity. The global greed that today is turning the Earth into a looted department store is rooted in this insanity. It is based on the loss of our sense of belonging to a community of life. This separation is the collective trauma of humanity. A huge amount of emotional suffering is due to our loss of community.

When the African cultural ambassador, Sobonfu Somé, travelled to the United States for the first time, and visited a family, she was surprised, and asked: "But where are all the others?" Yes, where are they — the neighbours, friends, sisters, uncles and aunts, nephews and nieces and companions who give our lives warmth, meaning and quality? Why have we banished so many opportunities for intimacy from our lives, so much contact, exchange, mutual assistance, cooperation, friction, feedback and learning from each other?

23

Historians can fairly precisely determine when the original tribes disappeared in each region. Broadly speaking, this coincided with the *Neolithic revolution,* when in many places at around the same time, a new kind of social organisation, based on ploughing land and the domestication of animals, arose and spread rapidly across much of the world. These new societies used violence and replaced complementarity and cooperation with command-and-control hierarchies.

This development in the way humans organised themselves in the world probably coincided with other changes in their inner development and self-organisation. We can speculate that the growing self-awareness of human beings at that time led to calls for societal forms to transform, so that people could find more freedom and liberation from established traditions and conventions. But instead of creating new forms of community, allowing for more individual expression, human beings turned to the rigidities of hierarchy and patriarchy and cut themselves off from community. This strategy did not bring the desired freedom — on the contrary: the human being created a prison of loneliness for himself.

If the longing for community remains unfulfilled, people often become members of fan clubs or cults instead and conform to views that, deep in their hearts, they do not really share. If isolated, a human being is ready to cross boundaries of good taste, common sense and compassion in order to somehow belong. Fascism used this fact mercilessly for its own purposes.

True community needs to sustain individual uniqueness and expression as well as a sense of belonging.

How do communities gain permanence?

Below, you will find some guiding ideas, not a methodology, on building permanence into communities. Ultimately, each community must find its own workable methods and refine them again and again, so that they remain alive. But there are some helpful experiences, some of which I would like to share here.

Community and individual

"Individuality... is a community endeavor" says the sociologist Dieter Duhm. Future communities are not characterised by conformity, but by pronounced individuality and diversity. In our communities we need to leave enough space for the development of the individual, enough time for being alone and for mutual recognition. We see how differences and diversity enrich our communities. We also recognise the difference between the I and the ego: whereas the ego separates, the I is always something that connects.

There is no functioning community without individuality. Conversely, there is no individuality without community: we cannot develop it alone behind closed doors; we need contact, feedback and friction to recognise who we are and to gain a sense of our strengths and weaknesses. The community can provide a safe place to find and speak our personal truth.

A common goal

There is no community where the members always like each other. It is like what happens in a personal relationship: when the initial infatuation subsides and the projections crumble, we must decide whether we wish to go our separate ways or find something that is stronger than momentary sympathy or antipathy. In the I Ching it says: "It is not the private interests of the individual that create lasting community, but rather the goals of humanity". Global compassion and a common goal with which the members can identify are essential. A strong bond arises among members when they notice that they complement each other and can trust each other in relation to the common goal.

Transparency and trust

Trust arises through transparency. It arises when you are seen in your innermost self and see the innermost self of the other. And that occurs when you show yourself. It is surprising what a heavy burden is lifted when you know that you don't have to fear being secretly judged and that the others will tell you if there is something about you they don't like. Instead of secret gossip, every community needs processes and methods to help make what is going on beneath the surface visible — all those things that are politely concealed and suppressed, but that ultimately pollute the atmosphere unless they are cleared out. Such a process needs to have its roots in humour, benevolence and human knowledge; it is not a question of hurting each other, but of showing oneself and understanding and liberating each other. Free expression, within a space where one does not need to worry about frightened or angry reactions from others, is liberating for every community.

25

Leadership structure and grassroots democracy

The role model for decision-making in community is no longer the pyramid, but the circle. The Native American Manitonquat writes: "In a circle, everyone is a leader. This means that everyone takes responsibility for the entire circle". Without participative decision structures, in which all voices are heard, no community will arise. But grassroots democracy requires mature people with leadership qualities, so that responsibility can truly be shared. And it requires human knowledge and the willingness to be transparent: so many agonising so-called objective debates can be seen to be sham fights once what is going on beneath the surface becomes visible. Ultimately, decisions should be made by those who are willing to take responsibility. To achieve this, and to move beyond the strict consensus model, many organisational tools have been developed in recent years.

Gender dynamics

Differences, attractions and misunderstandings between men and women create a dynamic in every community — it does no good to ignore it. So-called female qualities, such as care, empathy, compassion, pragmatism or the ability to listen — no matter whether they appear in men or in women — are essential elements in communities and are more in demand than in the normal business world. According to the Iroquois Constitution, a leader should be "like a good mother". Every community is only as good as its ability to honour the female qualities. And male qualities too, I would like to add: far-sightedness, strength of purpose, rationality, theory, drive — no matter whether they are found in men or women — are equally important for the ecovillage movement. A community needs to find ways of becoming aware of and balancing these qualities.

Most communities find men's and women's circles to be useful instruments for exchange, confirmation and a sense of home. Communities can embed lovers and families in a healing environment: in case of conflict, it helps to have friends who do not take sides with one or the other, but side with the love and truth between them.

Community of communities

Everything that has been said about individuals here is also true for communities in relationship to one another. In GEN (Global Ecovillage Network), we are in the midst of this process: individual communities open up to one another, recognise each other, become aware of how much they have in common — despite all their differences. It is especially the differences that provide great potential for communities to complement one another. They share their experiences and cooperate at an ever deeper level. From GEN conference to GEN conference we have observed how the communities let go of old competitive modes of behaviour and open up with their questions, issues and strengths and learn from each other. This process is far from complete — but already now we are benefiting from the diversity of this global family. Ecovillages in the North and the South are entering into committed partnerships of mutual assistance and responsibility. They take on their common challenges within their regions and work together with city planners, mayors and citizens' initiatives to stimulate their rural districts and make them sustainable. Ecovillages are seeing themselves less and less as individual phenomena, but increasingly as a part of a larger whole.

We call this whole the community of communities. This includes intentional communities and neighbourhood initiatives, traditional village communities, action groups for more democratic and ecological awareness, self-help groups in slums, eco-caravans and initiatives in refugee camps. Ultimately, it encompasses all groups and people who know that we can only achieve our goals together.

The Five Dimensions of Sustainability

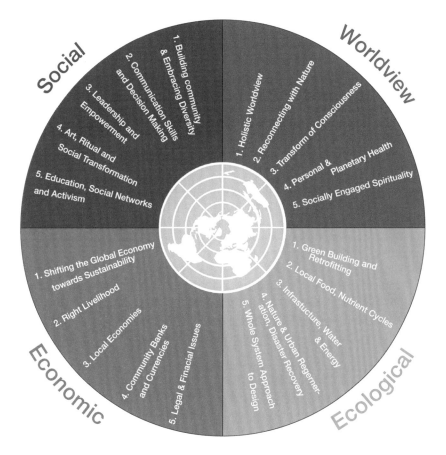

The Ecovillage Design Mandala was created by ecovillage educators in 2004, as the core symbol of the Ecovillage Design Education (EDE). It is a holistic map for sustainable design and development, embracing the social, worldview, ecological and economic dimensions of sustainability. The mandala can be applied to systems on all levels: to the life of an individual, an organisation, an intentional community, traditional village, urban neighbourhood, a region, etc. Over the years, integral or participatory design was clearly recognised as a fifth dimension and placed at the centre of the Mandala. In some contexts, the word 'worldview' is replaced by 'culture'.

Ecovillages have a wealth of experience, methods and tools to share in each of these five dimensions and the Solution Library is organised accordingly.

Culture and Worldview

Ecovillages grow within a wide variety of cultures, spiritual frameworks and worldviews, but some values are universal: the respect for life, inclusivity and embracing diversity, the cultivation of generosity and hospitality, openness to feedback, to name but a few. Responsibility and active care for the Earth and all its  inhabitants are the basis for a life-sustaining culture. This ethic transcends all cultures and religions.

Living in community is a permanent education, teaching us to relate to all life and to our self with more honesty and transparency. We learn to expand our responsibility (our ability to respond), our friendship and tolerance, even towards those beings who look, feel or think, very differently, or those who follow a different spiritual practice. Some individual ecovillages have been accused of being 'sects', because of their choice to explore a particular way of life that is different from the surrounding societal context. However, the simple fact that they form part of a rich and diverse, yet closely knitted, network through GEN, where they interact across all seeming divides with great openness and tolerance, points in the opposite direction. Cultural and spiritual diversity, like biodiversity, is a very precious resource on our journey into the future. Today, young people across the world can feel uncomfortable in their skins; they can feel too dark or too light, too fat or too slim. In GEN, we celebrate the beauty and wealth of diversity and cherish the gems of traditional wisdom that may hold seeds for a resilient future.

The Ecological Dimension

Ecovillages show that low-impact, high-quality lifestyles are possible: water, food, building materials and energy can be obtained in sufficient quantities in healthy regional cycles. In the Global South food and energy sovereignty are decisive factors for survival and freedom of choice. Cities can build healthy regional relationships and even surround themselves with an 'ecovillage belt'. More sustainable than suburbia by far! Replace those lawns with vegetable gardens!!

Energy autonomy: The ecological footprint of any community can be reduced substantially with ecological building techniques and thermal insulation, passive and active use of solar energy, as well as the replacement of energy-intensive forms of transport.

Water: Water consumption and sewage quantities can be reduced significantly by means of rainwater harvesting and storage, constructed wetlands for wastewater treatment, separation of drinking water and greywater, and compost toilets.

Food: Most ecovillages produce their own food and use their own fruit, vegetable, grain and animal products. The most important principles in this area are: companion planting, diversity, no artificial fertilisers or pesticides, use of own seeds and freshness.

Construction: An increase in the quality of life and environmental conservation is made possible by the use of regionally sourced, natural building and insulation materials such as clay, paper, straw and waste.

Waste: Nature's example is to be followed here as ecovillages reduce and eliminate their waste by means of closed cycles, composting and reusing.

Ecological footprint studies have been undertaken in ecovillages and some of the lowest footprints in the industrial world have been measured here.

29

The Social Dimension

Another vital factor in sustainability is the art of living and creating together: it is no use having the best farming or energy systems, organic houses and closed water and recycling cycles if we do not enjoy being together. Over the years, ecovillages and intentional communities have matured and become extremely skilful and experienced at communication, conflict facilitation, participatory decision-making, supporting individuals to find their place in the whole, and to thrive, healing past trauma and rebuilding trust. Communities have moved 'beyond consensus' to more refined structures that explore our capacity in human teams and organisations to become more than the sum of our parts, instead of meeting around the lowest common denominator. Collective wisdom is the new frontier: how can we truly pool our intelligence and intention in order to implement all the solutions we already hold in our hands and find those that are still needed?

The communities that overcame their crises and gained valuable experiences in doing so are now offering their knowledge to new initiatives.

The Economic Dimension

Fair, just, in solidarity, transparent, regenerative and interest-free — these are the hallmarks of a sustainable way of conducting business. Regional and local economic cycles need a corresponding finance system that retains value in the region.

Residents of ecovillages are conscious consumers, producers and traders — mainly of local goods. Within their community and in the region, they are establishing models for a new economy. Here small-scale economic experiments can take place, on the basis of trust and pioneering spirit: from communal savings cooperatives to regional currencies, from barter trade circles to community banks and gift economies.

There are many questions when it comes to the economic design of communities. And different ecovillages have found different answers. How is land ownership organised? Which legal forms work best? Should our businesses be run privately or cooperatively? Is work for the community paid? Do individuals have separate incomes or is income shared? Which funds are organised communally? How does the community care for its members when they are ill, or in old age? What happens when members of the community leave?

Regardless of the specific form a community chooses, trust, communication and close feedback loops are essential for the system to work.

Participatory or Integral Design

At the heart of what distinguishes ecovillages from mainstream communities lies a process of participatory design that gives ownership over the process to the inhabitants. Ecovillages cannot be designed by outside developers and architects, they spring from the dreams of the people and their wish to make a difference by taking their future into their own hands. Off course, the inhabitants can invite experts to support them in whatever way feels helpful. GEN has gained a rich experience in facilitating such communal design processes, and has professional teams on all continents. The EDE can be used to support such a design process.

The process starts by listening to the dreams and visions of the participants. What is the future they would like to see for their children? Then, they identify the strengths and weaknesses of their community/ village in each of the dimensions of the mandala. How connected are individuals to nature? How strong is the sense of self-worth and cultural celebration? How are conflicts dealt with? How is leadership shared? How are natural resources used and eco-systems regenerated? How sustainable are people economically? How could the environment be designed to support free energy flow and increased resilience on all levels? These and many more questions are with us as we explore together, whilst also allowing ourselves to be inspired by best-practice examples from all over the world.

The participants then go on to identify and design leverage points in each of the dimensions: steps can then be taken and projects can be realised, which will have a maximum impact for minimum effort. We start by harvesting the low-hanging fruits. An experience of success helps maintain momentum!

Within the group, we also find out who naturally takes responsibility for which parts of the emerging design, while at the same time giving everyone a sense of ownership over the whole process. Teams emerge that refine the designs for particular areas. These teams draw in others from the community to take implementation forward after the course. If any tensions arise these provide welcome input for the practice of conflict facilitation skills.

Through this process the web of mutual recognition and trust amongst participants is strengthened. Regular meetings take place to present the ensuing 'Community Resilience Plan', a living document, to further stakeholders.

EUROPE

The Stillness at the Centre

Findhorn / Scotland

One of the oldest ecovillages is Findhorn in Scotland, founded in 1962. Robin Alfred has had a leading position since 1995 and shares his story of the Findhorn Foundation.

Robin Alfred

Robin Alfred

It is the Wednesday evening of Experience Week. I am sitting in a circle with 15 other people, three men and twelve women, in the Beech Tree Room in Cluny Hill — one of the Findhorn Foundation's two main campuses. I look around the circle and feel love for everybody present. I have never felt quite like this before. In my 'normal' life in London I am a criminal justice social worker, highly opinionated and very politically engaged. I am a card-carrying member of the Labour Party and a member of every campaigning organisation I can lay my hands on, from the London Cycling Campaign to Amnesty and Greenpeace. The world is clearly separated into right-minded people like me and everybody else. Politics, personalities and personas separate me from most of the world. But at this moment in the Beech Tree Room I am connecting to something beyond the personality: a soft, sometimes covered and distant place that resides in the heart and soul of everyone. That evening in my journal I write 'Life will never be the same. I want to live in a place and in a way where I can continue to experience this unconditional love'.

What had drawn me to Findhorn was a leaflet handed to me by a homeopath I was seeing in London at that time. I knew very little about the Findhorn Foundation and went on a whim. Why not? However, most of the people drawn to my Experience Week were already aware of the dream and founding impulses of this amazing, internationally renowned 'intended but unintentional' community.

Foundation

On November 17th 1962 Eileen Caddy, Peter Caddy and Dorothy Maclean had towed their caravan and the three Caddy children to an inauspicious site in Findhorn Bay Caravan Park. They needed somewhere to live and the means to sustain them. In sandy soil, and embedded in an unfavourable climate, they began to garden. This, however, was no ordinary garden. Each of the three founders was already steeped in spiritual awareness. Eileen was a meditator, a member of the moral rearmament movement of the 1950s; Peter was a Rosicrucian and a practitioner of inspired, positive thinking; Dorothy had a background in Sufism, and had learnt the hard way to put God first in everything. Applying these spiritual principles both to the garden and to their lives as a whole, they began an experiment in co-creation — to live a life, where humanity, divinity and nature's intelligence were working together.

Over the next 50 years a community organically grew from these roots. The garden yielded legendary 40lb cabbages, which attracted both doubting scientists and spiritual seekers. Something interesting was clearly going on! The number of visitors grew and grew and soon required structured programmes and guest accommodation to hold them. An introductory Experience Week, the building of seven cedar wood bungalows, and in time the building of art studios, a community centre and, of course, a sanctuary followed.

Now we are a community of over 600: 120 coworkers in the Findhorn Foundation receiving food and accommodation and a small allowance for their service, and around 500 people living locally, drawn by the impulse seeded in 1962. We have the highest concentration of social enterprises in the UK (over 45 at the last count) and a vibrant community body, the New Findhorn Association, coordinating the community's activities. The Foundation itself, the charity at the heart of the community, now has over £5 million of assets, and an annual income of around £2 million. It provides personal development workshops and sustainability trainings, ranging in length from a few days to a few months, to over 2,000 people a year and has received countless awards as a workshop centre and honouring its built environment. Its ecological footprint is approximately half that of the UK national average and one of the lowest recorded in the Western world. The Foundation is also a recognised NGO of the United Nations, and Eileen Caddy received the Queen's MBE for her services to spiritual inquiry several years before her passing in 2006. A lot has transpired in these 50-60 years, including a conscious shift somewhere in the mid-1990s from being an 'alternative' to the mainstream to being 'complementary'. Partnerships now abound, and we are regularly consulted by local government, town planners, mayors and students about matters relating to sustainability and resilience.

*The Findhorn Garden was created out of cooperation between people
and nature beings and still attracts many guests
to the Findhorn community.*

Leadership Principles

During the four years following my Experience Week, I visited the Foundation a couple of times and in 1995 came to do a three-month arts programme and never left. Much to my surprise after eight months of working in the Park Homecare Department, learning to clean toilets and fold sheets with love and presence, I was asked to focalise the Foundation's reinvention process, looking at all the fundamentals of our community. Since then I have served in various leadership positions including Chair of

Management and Chair of the Board of Trustees. My learnings have been immense. In this article, I would like to focus on challenges and responses in the social and economic domains.

Peter, Dorothy and Eileen embodied three archetypes of leadership. Peter was a man of action, of focused will and intention — the masculine archetype. Eileen lived the feminine principle of receptivity and inner listening: 'Be still and know that I am God'; while Dorothy attuned to what she termed the Devas — intelligences that overlight different species and aspects of nature and humanity. The combination of these three principles lies not only at the heart of this community, but at the heart of any successful enterprise. Leadership is only effective when it can harness the masculine, the feminine and the co-creative principles.

One can track the rise and fall in fortune of this community by the presence or absence of these principles. Arguably Peter's and Dorothy's departure from the community in the 1970s, while Eileen remained resident, has meant that the feminine principle of listening to the 'still small voice within' lives most strongly in the community. Dorothy´s return to the community in 2009 led to renewed enthusiasm for the application of the principles of co-creation with nature. Rightly or wrongly many have bemoaned the lack of the masculine energy. Certainly as a leader I found the need to cloak my masculine drive with as much feminine grace and subtlety as I could muster. At times, we are more gifted at developing appropriate processes and nurturing healthy relationships than achieving the task.

One of the many ways the feminine principle manifests is in the desire to sit in circles and reach consensus in decision-making. We have come a long way from the mythical days when 300 people needed to agree the colour of the new carpet in the Cluny Dining Room but decision-making is still a long and complex process. We have seen the benefit of mandating smaller groups to make decisions in the areas for which they are responsible. We have also learnt about the tyranny of the naysayer and have developed decision-making processes that go beyond seeking unanimity. Asking those who disagree with a proposal if they are willing to be 'a loyal minority', i.e. someone who disagrees with a decision but will not sabotage its implementation, is a helpful way to build consensus when unanimity is not possible. More recently we have started to work with Sociocracy, seeking consent rather than consensus.

Economy

On the economic front, like many ecovillages and also like many who live in this part of Scotland, we are continually challenged. The Foundation survives largely because its members are willing to work, in essence, as volunteers while affluence in the wider community is also difficult to achieve. Our responses to this have been several:

- In 2001 we created Ekopia, an Industrial Provident Society that serves as a vehicle for ethical investment in the community. At the time of writing there is around £1 million invested in a range of community projects including the Moray Steiner School, Findhorn Wind Park and the Phoenix Community Stores.

- In 2002 we created our own currency, the Eko, issued by Ekopia and redeemable on a £1 for 1 Eko basis. While small in value (around 20,000 Ekos are circulating at any one time) the Eko serves to stimulate local trading and raise awareness that every time we shop we vote. Shopping locally helps build a diverse and more economically sustainable community.

- Lastly and most importantly, from the very earliest days of the community, we work with the Laws of Manifestation, codified in the 1970s by David Spangler. In essence this means that if we tune in to what the universe wants to happen and focus our inner work to align with that intention, then the resources to realise these projects are more likely to be manifested. From the construction of the art studios, Community Centre and Universal Hall in the 1970s, through the purchase of the Caravan Park in 1983, to the more recent manifestation of the widely acclaimed Moray Art Centre, stories of these laws in action are legion. 'Do what you love and the money will come', or 'Feel the fear and do it anyway' are everyday descriptions of these same laws in action. It is impossible to think of the Findhorn Foundation's unfolding history in the absence of the application of this core principle. It is important to note that this is not the same as simply saying you will get whatever you wish for. Your wishes need to be in tune with what God or Spirit wills.

37

After 5 years' working in the heart of the community, while living in a romantic, funky and mould-ridden caravan in the Pineridge area of The Park, I moved to rent a home in nearby Findhorn Village. Eileen, who I have been blessed to count as a dear friend and mentor, told me I was 'taking an outbreath'. It felt like that. I became one of about a dozen non-resident coworkers, receiving a minimum wage salary but being responsible for my own home, energy bills and food, while still working full-time for the Foundation. This trend, particularly for longer-term Foundation members, is very much alive.

The Universal Hall of the Findhorn Foundation, a meeting point for visionaries and committed people worldwide.

Exhale

In conclusion, what interests me most about the four dimensions of the ecovillage, a concept that, if not created here it was certainly pioneered here by John Talbott and others, is not so much the brilliance of identifying the social, economic, environmental and cultural dimensions to sustainability, but attending to the stillness at the centre from which they all derive. In the words of Eileen Caddy:

> *"Do you want to do something to help the world situation? Then look within. As you change your consciousness to love, peace, harmony and unity, the consciousness of the whole world will change."*

www.findhorn.org

> Keywords for Solution Library:
> Living Machine — designing sustainable wastewater treatment systems for urban settings
> Tuning In — supporting communities and groups to coalesce around clear intention
> The Laws of Manifestation — using clear intention as a tool for manifestation
> *solution.ecovillage.org*

A Community of Foster Families

Kitezh / Russia

Kitezh is a community and ecovillage dedicated to the nurturing of foster children. Andrew Aikman first heard of Kitezh in 1994 and first visited the community in 2006. He has lived there ever since, teaching English, working as a carpenter in the workshop and supervising Western volunteers.

Andrew Aikman

Andrew Aikman

Kitezh is a hamlet, around 360 km south of Moscow, surrounded by forests and close to the small village of Chumazovo. A lake lies between Kitezh and Chumazovo, covered with bright green weeds in spring, and sealed over by half a metre of ice in the winter. The hamlet consists of just over sixteen houses, a school, a workshop, and several outbuildings, including a cowshed. Though its 'footprint' is naturally small, ecological sustainability is not the first priority.

In the latter days of the Soviet Union a well-known correspondent for Mayak Radio in Russia, Dmitry Morozov, observed the plight of street children, living without the support of parents in his country. The Soviet Union fell apart, and with it the ideals of communism. Morozov, well educated and travelled, did not see mainstream Western values as a better alternative. So in those chaotic post-Soviet years, he set out to create a community that offered a different way of life, aspiring to the best of human values.

Morozov used his opportunity as a broadcaster to air his views and ask for support. The response was heartening. Many people started visiting the area. The local government in the Kaluga region saw their chance to polish their image: "Lets offer him a patch of land here; it'll look good for us. His scheme is likely to fail anyway, and we'll get the land back again." That was in 1992. Kitezh is still here, and now very much supported by the new regional governor. In the early days there were of course suspicions and mistrust, but good relationships have been fostered by openness; by inviting local, regional and eventually national officials and workers in the same field (education and social work), to visit Kitezh and see what happens here.

At the beginning there were no inside toilets, and the winter temperatures fall to -30°C. The pioneers, almost entirely city people from many walks of life, built the houses and the school of Kitezh by hand, summer and winter, sustained by the salary of Morozov and donations of well-wishers. These were times of optimism, idealism, very hard work and humour. As the doctor, Marina, a sophisticated Muscovite, recalls, "I came in my long coat, and my elegant white gloves, and Morozov looked me up and down and thought, 'she won't last the winter'. Well, I've been here seventeen years now."

*The ecovillage Kitezh has given homes to children without parents
and to their foster families.*

A Home for Social Practices

The care and nurture of children is the purpose of life in Kitezh. Officially, Russia has about 700,000 'social orphans'. Their biological parents are often still living but have, usually because of alcoholism, been declared unfit to parent their children. "Sometimes my mum didn't come home for days and there wasn't anything to eat in the house. I went to my gran's and she fed me. When my mum came home, gran shouted at her, but it didn't make any difference." Every nation has its social casualties.

The community, now led by Maxim Aneekiev, helps children adapt to everyday life, to overcome their trauma and pain. Children learn, not by listening to adults, but by exploring a therapeutic environment of challenges, care and love. The quality and inner world that adults bring help to create and influence this environment. As Morozov commented, "perhaps it would be best to develop the adults first, before they work with the children. In reality, though, they develop alongside the children. This is the natural way. Through the reflective awareness of the reality of everyday activity… adults understand the necessity to change and work with their own attitude towards life. By helping others they are helping themselves."

Learning Through Playing

There are regular 'awareness' meetings, when children gather in small groups and talk about what they have learned and understood about life in the last few days. It might be the beauty of a moonlit night, or the feeling of pain or joy when a child thinks about some past event. Thus they learn to understand themselves and what their feelings tell them. Kitezh has an excellent theatre director. Through acting, 'pretending' to be someone else, children learn about themselves, and how they are 'playing' their own character. Especially during the first month and throughout the year, there are kafchek evenings. The word means 'ark' as in Noah's ark, the place of safety. Children choose adults they want to meet — not their (foster) parents — and spend an hour or so having tea, getting to know them, discovering each other as real people.

In this therapeutic environment, the world isn't split up into insulated segments of school, home, medical services, private/social life and so on. The community is the social workers, who are also the teachers, the parents, the psychologists, and all! Children know their teachers, for they are the parents, or parents of friends. In the words of Maxim Anikeev: "We are building an educational system drawing on the interests of the child. The teachers must be flexible and empathetic with their needs. Teaching and nurturing our children is the business of all adult residents of the village, including the bus driver and the cook. All questions are relevant, how and when to run the lessons, whether to do homework in groups or individually, how to draw out the strengths of the children, fill in the gaps in their knowledge... to replace 'scars' with a proper appraisal of successes and failures."

For a child that did not experience love and care as an infant, love-deficit can easily become a black hole, which may never be filled. Here the strength of the community of foster parents comes into its own. Once a child has joined our family (the community), there is no 'giving up'. The burden is shared, but so are the joys. There are many difficult issues as our fostered children adapt to socially acceptable behaviour, e.g. not stealing. In orphanages, taking what you can is a survival mechanism; there's never enough. And hoarding is security. Stealing and hoarding are effective survival behaviour. As one boy put it, "having to beg is so shameful!"

When I was learning to be a teacher, we were told, 'don't give the children your heart, they will take it and break it'. Here, in Kitezh, we give the children our hearts but within the united strength of a community. The teenager who 'hates' his parents can find another family in the village until the storm has passed — usually after a few months. Foster parents focus on frequent and explicit demonstrations of their love for the teenager. Occasionally, after completing school, a young adult remains within the safety of the community for a while, working as a volunteer, in the kitchen, or the garden or the farm, while we wait for them to grow, emotionally, into full maturity and readiness to leave. The therapeutic structure of Kitezh is referred to as 'The Game'. Drama and opportunity are interwoven into a series of flexible but increasingly challenging steps, leading the child towards self-responsible adulthood.

In the community, children and youth are learning to trust again,
to speak their truth and to share.

Justice

The weekly meetings help bind the community together. Beginning with greeting each other, we recognise who is there, who is not. Then, the week's diary: for fostered children, unpredictability equals fear, they need to know what and who to expect. Next, the 'business': anyone, from the youngest to the oldest can bring up any issue in the knowledge that they will be listened to, and taken seriously. For instance, the children might say: "The dishwasher doesn't work properly." "Who is looking after the chickens?" or "Can we play the game of 'secret friend'"? All such questions are resolved by community discussion, not by the adult minority. Then we discuss who has achieved which steps in 'The Game' , and what we are looking forward to? Lastly, thanks — a sharing of appreciation, and all end with a moment of silence.

Justice, too, is a very public concern. Anyone can call for justice, and The Court seeks to find 'resolution', not retribution. Often offenders, when they have accepted their 'offence', make amendments in the form of work or giving back. But this too is with their agreement and acceptance. The very public nature of the court helps many to understand the implications of their own behaviour. However, fostering siblings presents its own problems: when the values of Kitezh and those of the 'family clan' conflict, the child will almost always stick with the clan. Sonya was a small child when she came to Kitezh with her many siblings. As she grew and continued to reject our way of life, we realised that her agreement to live here was primarily a choice to remain with her siblings. So we asked an orphanage to take her in for a couple of weeks, so that she could look at her situation, and make a real choice to live in Kitezh, or not. She decided to come back and, especially once all her older siblings had left, we saw real change.

Expanding

The work of Kitezh has become better known in the region and in Moscow through the Role Play Games run during the holidays. These events, lasting up to two weeks, are designed to help children confront their own issues with courage, and with the support of their friends. Through these public events, Kitezh has expanded to take in children who come from 'good families', but are not thriving in normal school in the city.

From the early days of Kitezh, there have been meaningful international connections, beginning with Liza Hollingshead and Ecologia Youth Trust from Findhorn in Scotland. In 1995, the first group of young people from abroad came to experience Russia and taste the Kitezh way of life. With the continued help of Ecologia Youth Trust, Kitezh runs a programme for international volunteers to spend up to three months experiencing and supporting our work. We receive students of Russian language and culture, youth groups from America, Canada and England, and older individuals interested in our work.

Kitezh has been the subject of many short television items and articles in the press. Dmitri Morozov has received national recognition for his work and Maxim Anikeev has published a number of papers and gives lectures on the nurturing of disadvantaged children.

http://en.kitzesh.org

Keywords for Solution Library:

Schooling without Fear — educating children in a compassionate way

The Self-Empowerment Game — challenging adolescents to grow their self-esteem

solution.ecovillage.org

Balancing Individuality and Community

Damanhur / Italy

Damanhur is a Federation of 26 communities located in Piedmont, Northern Italy which explore different aspects of ecovillage life. Damanhur has its own currency and an in-depth cultural identity. Humour, the joy of art and creativity, clear organisational structures, and plenty of work are the main features of Damanhur.

Formica Coriandolo and Macaco Tamerice

Macaco Tamerice*

As a jazz singer I was very successful in Japan. Once success and career became my reality, I knew I no longer wanted to live in this world of illusions. 22 years ago I decided to move to Damanhur. I had always thought that for a person like me, with a strong sense of individuality, living in community would be impossible. I soon realised however that I was much happier in community than ever before.

Formica Coriandolo*

31 years ago I lived with friends in the historic part of Florence. I owned a motorbike, had a great job, but felt like I was missing something. Then I watched a TV programme about Damanhur: an interview with its founder Falco. He spoke of solidarity, about helping one another, and about spiritual and human values and deep connections to nature — completely different subjects from mainstream life in Italy. I drove to Damanhur.

Founder

Oberto Airaudi — or 'Falco' — came from Balangero in the province of Turin. From a young age, he had experiences with the paranormal. Together with a group of friends, he felt the urge to start a community. A group of 12 people gave up their homes and jobs and began a 2-year search all around the world for the right place. A location was found 40 kms outside Turin at a nodal point of four Synchronic Lines (lines of power throughout the planet, described in the ancient science of geomancy). This is where Damanhur was later founded. The landowner welcomed this group with the words: "What has taken you so long? I have been waiting quite some time for you." Many years ago this landowner had dreamt that young people, with the wish to change the world, would come to buy his land. That's when Damanhur began.

Functions of Communities

Today Damanhur has around 1,000 inhabitants, including children. We live across 26 communities, also called nucleos, of 15 to 25 people each. Each nucleo has a territory, a piece of land, and a specific function for Damanhur. For instance, our nucleo, Dendera, connects to GEN and the other communities in the world. The neighbouring nucleo is involved in experimentation with water, energy and sustainability. One nucleo focuses on agricultural self-sufficiency, another takes care of the Temple, yet another of guests and hospitality, etc. Every community conducts research within a specific field, and shares the results of its research with all the others. In nearly all our communities, elders, adults and children live together. Every nucleo has a garden, an alternative energy source, greenhouses and animals.

The nucleos build the human base or fundament within Damanhur. Here we know each other intimately, we eat together, we live together and it is here that most conflicts arise. Conflicts rarely happen about major topics in Damanhur. It seems like a paradox, but it's easier if they occur in the areas of washing up or doing laundry. We do not fear conflicts:

we understand that the experience of reality differs amongst individuals depending on personality and cultural background. That´s why, in a conflict, we do not look at who is right or wrong, but rather for solutions that could work for all involved parties.

For the management of Damanhur all the Damanhurians elect two people every six months who are called king and queen guides. They are not like royalty; these titles came about during a playful period in Damanhurian history and have remained since then. We like to be playful!

Four Pillars

Damanhur rests on four pillars that inspire and regulate the different levels of our life. Each pillar has different solutions and strategies to ultimately serve the same goal. Each is equally respected:

- *School of Meditation* is the first pillar and has spiritual evolution as its clear goal. Meditation has a unique position in the community of Damanhur.

- *Social Life* includes the entire management of co-living, and of everyday life.

- The third pillar, *Game of Life*, represents the power of transformation. Transformation is part of our philosophy: fear of change prevents people living a full and happy life. If we wait until something really doesn't work any more, we waste too much energy. This is why we change things before problems arise. Everyone is invited to offer solutions and propose changes. The Game of Life uses creative and unusual strategies to encourage people to get out of their usual habits. It can lead to great action. For example, a few years ago, we created the *Battle of the Arts*, and made many collective works of art that transformed Damanhur.

- The fourth pillar, *Tecnarcato*, is a system used for transformational work on a personal level. For example, if I am an aggressive or shy person, I can find support and strategies that may assist. Tecnarcato uses many methods, e.g. I choose another person whom I trust, and this person works with me to set up a programme of self-transformative steps that help me to change my habits and limitations. We all wish to develop and express our highest potential.

47

The underground 'Temple of Humankind' is a masterpiece of art and was kept secret for many years. Today it is an attraction point for visitors from around the world.

Art and the Spiritual Vision of Damanhur

In Damanhur we believe that human beings have a divine origin. That each of us carries a divine spark that can be reawakened. This is the goal of Damanhur. We can accelerate the process of our evolution if we work collectively. Art is seen as an essential instrument for expressing our divine creative potential. We are often taught as children to say and to think: 'I cannot do this!' Yet everyone is capable of using creative energy to make something unique. This is the primary power of the arts: to bring forth the uniqueness within us. Art is a bridge, a language. We usually think that languages exist as words. Yet art can transmit information and emotions in a much more complete and tangible way through other senses and channels. Collective art creates a strong sense of unity while expressing individual diversity. Just like in indigenous cultures, for us, art is a language that creates a common identity.

Temple of Humankind

Like many groups, the founders of Damanhur wished to have a sacred place. The idea of an underground temple, an expression of divine creativity, had fascinated Falco since childhood, and one night, the community began digging with shovels and spades. They dug in secrecy for 16 years, reaching 80 meters down into the mountain, without building permission. We called the space the Temple for Humankind, and meant to unveil it to the public after completion. But it happened otherwise.

A former member of Damanhur started to blackmail us, asking for money in order to keep the secret of the Temple. We denied his request

48

and he went public. Then, 40 policemen came to Damanhur and said: "If you do not show us the temple, we will blow up the entire mountain." The magistrate was expecting to find drugs and weapons. After we took him on a tour through the Temple, adorned with beauty and art, his eyes were filled with tears. He declared that he would take the Temple under his personal care. But still, local officials planned to fill the Temple with sand. In order to protect what we had created, we went public and collected 100,000 signatures and worked on a policy proposal to legalise underground buildings. A year later, in Rome, the Ministry of Cultural Heritage declared the Temple as a Work of Art.

This was an unbelievable joy for us. In Damanhur we know: any circumstance that appears to be catastrophic can be transformed for the better. What I love about Damanhur is that feeling that 'Nothing is impossible!' If you have a dream, you can realise it. And you can always count on the help of others, on their solidarity and support.

Strengths and Weaknesses

The complexity of Damanhur is our strength, but it can also become our weakness. Our philosophy expresses itself through doing, in action. We want to bring our creativity into the world fully. We lead rich and busy lives, including the practical concern of making a living. The majority of Damanhurians work in Damanhurian companies and organisations, whilst others work outside the community. I, Macaco, am a singing teacher in Turin, not just to earn money but because I love singing. Additionally, I work as a representative for Damanhur in GEN. Beyond this we also have many other responsibilities, like service in our nucleos, work on the land, taking care of children, etc. I wish we had more time for doing everything. We have not found a way to simplify our lives and also take care of the many responsibilities.

Falco's Death

We are a community with a founder who had a very clear vision. In such communities there lies a risk that after the founder's death everything collapses. In Damanhur this was not the case. In winter 2012, Falco was diagnosed with cancer. He decided to use natural therapies and not to undergo chemotherapy. He used every moment of his remaining time, three more months of life, to prepare for his departure, conversing with Damanhurians, leaving things so they could continue serenely without him. In those months, he was more present than ever, and he was teaching and speaking in public until his final days.

When Falco died, all of Damanhur felt the loss deeply. We became aware of how much responsibility we each carry. We came together more fully as a community. Even now, we sometimes read what Falco wrote shortly before his passing, messages with the intention of keeping our motivation high and also reminding us of the love he felt. In these years, Damanhur has been newly re-organised, and each one of us gives our very best to realise our shared dreams. We are in the process of transforming Damanhur more deeply than ever before, as a living piece of art!

www.damanhur.org

* In Damanhur, a citizen's first name is that of an animal, and their last name is that of a plant

Art and Spirituality have a deep meaning for the people of Damanhur.

Keywords for Solution Library:

Game of Life — ensuring that the structures of a community remain alive and creative

Feedback and Personal Growth — utilising the feedback of others to refine one´s personality

Community Currency — strengthening localisation of wealth

solution.ecovillage.org

Reclaiming Freedom, Empowerment and Sustainability

Lakabe / Spain

The community of Lakabe started as a social activist group, after the long Spanish dictatorship under Franco, with the vision of creating a life without violence in an abandoned village in Navarra. After 35 years, having passed through many phases and crises, it is an ecovillage with 53 members demonstrating a whole variety of sustainable solutions. Mauge Cañada has been there at different stages of her life.

Mauge Cañada

Mauge Cañada

In 1979, at the age of 19, I was sharing a house with friends in Bilbao. Sharing and connecting has always been a base of my life. I never thought that for me there could be a life without community. I was also an activist against military service — part of the first pacifist group in the country. We succeeded, the law was changed, and people all over Spain were no longer obliged to do military service. After this success, we decided to take another step and try to live a life without violence. With this as our motivation, our group rented a house in the countryside.

We had goats. And one day, searching for our lost goats, we found an abandoned village in the forest — Lakabe. It was abandoned because there was no road leading there. We fell in love with it. In meetings with groups of activists from all over Spain — Andalucía, Cataluña, Madrid — we decided to occupy this village. We invited anyone who wanted to live an experimental life of nonviolence to join us on 21st March 1980. A lot of people came. In that year I gave birth to my two daughters, so I joined a year later.

During the first 2 years, people were coming and going. No one had money, so we built with what we found. We carried cement by hand, walking for hours through the woods. It was heavy, but we were full of hope. We had a lot of help from the many people that came. Once we had horses and donkeys, we could access the village much more easily. We had a lot of fun with theatre and music, and looking at the photos of that time, you would think that there were only parties. The sensation of freedom was amazing. It was like, 'Wow! Everything we had dreamt about was possible'. We were very young, and we were coming from the experience of a dictatorship and its repressive atmosphere that had ended only a few years before. We were in a radical empowerment process.

Difficulties

Still, when dreams become reality, not everything is easy. Sometimes there were roses, other times, thorns. Having to manage the growing community was tough. We had many idealistic ideas, but once we entered the reality of governance and decision-making, it was very difficult. Endless assemblies and meetings were held. Anyone who showed up at the community could say whatever they wanted, and the ones who spoke most had a lot of power.

During one assembly in 1981, when I was 21 years old and had two babies, a part of the group said they didn't really want children or dogs. It was painful for me to see the group so out of touch with reality. There were conflicts between those who wanted to live in austerity, and others who wanted a good quality of life. The battle between those who were against machines and wanted to use axes for woodcutting, and those who wanted to use chainsaws cost us months of time. Then some people said 'we will use only candles', and others said 'no, we are allowed torches with batteries'. Lastly, there were those who were against everything, on principle. Now we can laugh about it, but back then it was really hard. I became more and more concerned.

The shift came when our connection to nature deepened. We were all coming from city life, but after a while, we began to reconnect to nature — a beautiful discovery. We understood that living in a rural setting required care for our environment. We began to develop our ecological awareness and started putting it into action. We decided to build a wind turbine. The steel base of it was 10 m long. 35 people carried this huge object through the forest and up the tracks to Lakabe. When we had finally done it, we felt we had just achieved the impossible.

The village of Lakabe was abandoned when the young community pioneers found it and built new homes from its ruins.

53

Change

In the first ten years we rebuilt the old village completely and learned to create community. What we explored and experienced during these ten years became the basis for all further development. All the agreements we reached in those first ten years still stand today, after 35 years.

Life in Lakabe is very intense as the community works as a collective: our work, our money, our decisions — everything is shared. Crises in our history always came up when part of the group wanted to put more power and energy into personal issues and interests. Our biggest crisis has gone down in our history as **The Crisis of '91**. People left; from more than 50 inhabitants we shrank to only 20. The amount of energy we had put in had exhausted us. More and more people needed to prioritise their personal lives and focus on their own motivation. It was a difficult moment for everybody — both for the people who left and the people who stayed in the community. I was among those who left. It was necessary for me to confront myself with what I wanted in life. I began training and became a therapist, but also went through therapy myself, trying to understand what happens when you live in a community. I was also taking more responsibility for my two children who were growing up and needed other things. Later I came back, but at this time I left.

Throughout those years, I never lost contact with Lakabe. Our agreements made it possible for the community to survive. Luckily we had written them down. A lot of clarity arose from them, and in the end the crisis turned out to be very positive; out of it grew more clarity about our identity.

During the 90s, those at Lakabe started exploring the inner side of community. We also started taking more care of our children and their growing needs.

Living in Lakabe has been an intensive community experience, sharing all aspects of life.

Photo: Leila Dregger

The Dam

At this point another incident happened: a Spanish company planned to build a reservoir dam for electricity production, and all the villages around were threatened with flooding. Lakabe was heavily involved in the protests against this project. Through this, we opened up to our neighbours and other movements. With a lot of energy from the community, using non-violent action, we tried to stop this project. Many activists ended up in jail. Still, we didn't succeed.

Lakabe is so high it was not flooded. But it was very, very painful to witness the destruction of the villages in the valley. Even now, 15 years after, I feel pain about this atrocity. It got stuck in the souls of the people concerned. It was one of the saddest moments of my life when the bulldozers came. The police allowed me to go to a village to see what was happening. I remember an old house of hundreds of years with flowers on the terrace and two old people coming out — and bulldozers destroying this — it is a horrible memory, to this day, I won't walk there.

One of the side effects of the dam was that a new road was built to Lakabe. We never wanted it. For us it destroyed the silence of the mountains. But some of our visitors were happy.

During the resistance, we had reached out to everyone in the region. In the beginning we were seen as hippies, but now we were respected by the surrounding villages because of our leading role in the resistance. The region sees us as a group that has something to offer. Members from Lakabe have been elected to the local council of our valley. A member from Lakabe, Mabel Cañada, has been elected as head of waste management in the wider region. She is bringing all her knowledge on how to reuse and recycle garbage. Her presence has a huge impact, and her example is changing the minds of people in similar positions. They are making a garbage revolution now!

Lakabe Today

In the history of Lakabe it was very important to get involved in RIE (Iberican Network) and in GEN. This helped us to understand that we are part of something bigger. Things become clearer when you see your position within a movement. It is like a field of resonance.

Today, we have three generations living in Lakabe. We are 100% self-sufficient in energy. In terms of food, we have 80% regional food sovereignty. People come and do trainings and workshops here to learn about this kind of life. We have our own school. Our children show what Lakabe is about. They have a strong sense of social behaviour and are very committed to understanding what is taking place on the planet.

We have worked a lot on governance and decision-making and offer workshops throughout Spain to help people set up proper governance in their projects and communities. We advise them to set up various working groups with decision-making power, so that fewer decisions need to pass through a general assembly, and to complete every decision-making process with a proper agreement document. It is important for the process to be inclusive, clear, transparent, and to arrive at a happy ending.

We also developed a mature emotional sharing process. When we meet, we begin by sharing, even if it is not easy. And should a situation require deeper attention, we form a support group. We have a rich toolbox of very diverse methodologies and approaches, depending on what is needed.

New communities and other projects are now growing out of Lakabe. One year ago, I myself was involved in developing a new community, Arterra Bizimodu, half an hour from Lakabe. We received help from the community of Lakabe, and now Arterra is flowering and even hosting an office of GEN-Europe. Meanwhile, based on their own experience, some of the youth of Lakabe are rebuilding another abandoned village.

The most important thing for me about Lakabe is to show that 'Yes, we can!' Yes, we can create new lifestyles, instead of blindly following the mainstream. Yes, we realise our dreams. Yes, we can live in community!

Keywords for Solution Library:

Recycling Oil — reducing waste
Good Governance — implementing successful decision making processes

solution.ecovillage.org

Building Bridges Between Cities and Villages

Güneşköy / Turkey

In fast developing Turkish society, the ecovillage project of Güneşköy, situated 65 km from Ankara, aims to overcome the cultural and economic gap between village and city. The project is offering small farmers an opportunity to sell products directly in city markets. This enables them to show-case sustainable solutions in organic cultivation while also empowering women. The win-win situation helps to conserve nature and village life. Ali and İnci Gökmen, Professors of Chemistry from Ankara, have for many years spoken out for nature and community.

Ali Gökmen

Ali Gökmen

My connection to nature started when I was three years old. My family had a vineyard on the edge of Ankara. At that time, the gardens were full of fruit trees and when blossoming, the whole region turned white. My grandmother used to wake me up before prayers to go out and pick fruits and grapes. Today, the same area is covered with apartment buildings and the trees have been cut down. After university I went travelling, and whilst visiting the mountains I once again found my connection to nature. What

I love most in my life is that, in İnci, I have a partner who enjoys the same things as myself. Our partnership is the smallest community, from this space it can grow.

Inci Gökmen

İnci Gökmen

There were four girls and one boy in my family. However, for dinner there were always ten to fifteen people around our table. All friends were welcome, creating a community in our home. I have enjoyed being with people and sharing ever since. Today, Ali and I teach chemistry at the University of Ankara. However, I place most value on knowledge that is not found in books. Experience, passed on amongst friends or shared from one generation to another, creates community. Even in the worst situations, there is always a solution to be found. I believe many problems grow from the disconnection we have from community and nature.

Development Destroys Villages and Nature

Turkey has been hit by a global trend: 'development and modernisation'. Our national GDP has grown immensely in the last years. Meanwhile, Turkish culture with its village life and urban communities culture, with city parks and fresh food, is disappearing rapidly. All the high-rise buildings in Ankara's centre have been built in the past five to ten years. The car industry is booming. Millions of trees are being cut down. It seems we don't think about the ecological consequences. Water, soil, trees, air have no monetary value. Thousands of dams are being built everywhere in the country. Rivers are being sold to investors. In the past, farmers could use water freely for irrigation, now water must be paid for. 'Development', as implemented in Turkey, is destroying village life. Many farmers were left with only one choice: to join the workforce of the mining industry. In 2014 a new law was passed that declared villages are no longer to be villages, instead making them into districts of nearby cities.

The plan to build a shopping mall in Gezi Park in Istanbul in 2013 was the straw that broke the camel's back. A handful of young people camped there to protect the trees, and then the protests exploded. Millions of people all around Turkey took to the streets for many weeks. The response of officials was very violent. Through the use of tear gas and rubber bullets several people died and hundreds were wounded.

However, we are still hopeful. We believe that we can create a world where all people have jobs, not by cutting down trees but by planting trees. Words alone do not convince people. We need local examples and good working models as centres of inspiration. By focusing on marrying our love for our culture with our love for the future, the current system will become obsolete.

The days of the ecovillage are limited: soon a high-speed train will be built here, destroying the valley.

Güneşköy, the Sunvillage

The founder of the Turkish state, Atatürk, said, "The villagers are the actual owners of this country." However, over the last fifty years, being a villager is considered something lowly. This has to change. The farmers produce the food and take care of nature. If they abandon this, the cities will be hungry. We wanted to create a project that helps people to stay in the villages, and that reconnects urban and rural inhabitants through direct economic links. Building bridges between cities and villages changes the awareness of all. We found land which was 65 km from Ankara, near a traditional village, Hisarköy. We founded a cooperative, calling it Güneşköy-Sunvillage. The land was owned by the state, but villagers were using it for grazing animals. We had several meetings with the villagers to gain their consent. Life in Turkish villages is very traditional. Although Güneşköy is only one hour from Ankara, the villagers regarded us as foreigners.

It took us two years to prepare this wild piece of land. University students and people with their children came to help. After some time, we found that the well we had been using had been demolished, and it seemed clear that the local villagers had done this. We understood that they were acting from a sense of scarcity — not wanting us — as newcomers — to use their water. Water is a critical issue in Turkey and is shared carefully by the inhabitants of any one place. Any newcomer claiming water could mean that the villagers have less of this precious good. So, we did not argue, and drilled a new well on one of our neighbour's properties, thus finding a good solution to the problem.

Agricultural Solidarity

We tried to convince local farmers to adopt organic farming. We ran information meetings with villagers in the coffeehouse, arguing against the use of chemicals. They listened politely but didn't try it themselves. In 2005, when we started our own organic agriculture on the land, we produced a lot of broccoli. We tried to take it to the local market to sell. But the price was so low it wasn't worth it. We then decided to give the broccoli away as gifts, having such abundance. However, this wasn't a good role-model for local farmers, given that agriculture is their income.

In 2006, we started a Community Supported Agriculture (CSA) scheme in Ankara. In the first year more than ninety people joined. We collected money to employ a farmer from the village and introduced him to new techniques: raised beds and drip irrigation. The villagers were still using the traditional irrigation method of flooding the fields, which uses a lot of water. We distributed vegetables with a van throughout Ankara. Interest was high and we were happy. The economic success convinced villagers to try organic farming too! Their minds started to change. Today, many families bring their produce to the organic market in Ankara. The people in the city buy at a fair price. Both sides are happy.

Women's Situation

We asked two women from the neighbouring village to work on our land: Fatma, aged fifty, and Seda, aged thirty-five. They were the first women from the village to ever work for money. The men in the village criticised it, but the women didn't listen to them. Traditional village life places a heavy burden on women: work in the fields, raising children, preparing and conserving food whilst looking after animals. Many men sit in a café throughout the day. That is why many young women no longer want to marry village boys.

Seda is a widow, and Fatma's decision is supported by her husband. Earning money is a revolution for them. They are being acknowledged for what they've been doing for generations. For them freedom has started with being paid for work. Now, they go together to the market and sell directly, which is a new life for them — not just because of the money but because of the contact with city people.

Fatma: "The women in town sometimes tell me I should look after myself more; I look older than I am. I tell them: What do you want? I really know how to use myself. I am not like a dress only made for the cupboard."

Seda: "We feed the city people, and they should know our value. They should visit our places to appreciate what we do for them."

They know how important it is to build trust with clients.

Fatma: "We never cheat in the organic market; the clients will know it and never buy again."

Whenever we visit them we never leave without being invited to try their homemade bread, cheese and fresh herbs, and receiving buckets full of fresh food and seeds to take home.

Learning and Experimenting

On the site, we constructed our first building out of mud bricks. Our neighbours taught us how to build in this local traditional way, using special soil. Next, we built a straw bale house. It was a huge learning experience for all of us, working with fifty to sixty volunteers at weekends. We thought it would be built in a month, but in the end it took six months, as we kept finding problems and discovering new solutions. In co-operation with the Department of Agriculture, we created a big greenhouse, using solar energy and extending the growing season by growing plants earlier in spring and later in the autumn.

People are now visiting us, learning from us and initiating ecovillage projects in other locations. Organic farming in Turkey is spreading at last. Today eight organic markets have been established in Istanbul, and two in Ankara. We have offered three Ecovillage Design Education (EDE) courses at the university and several of the participants started working in sustainability related areas. One group started a 'Sustainable Living Film Festival'. For seven years they have had a three-day festival with films, discussions and other activities. This year, they went on to launch a Sustainable Living TV channel.

The core of Güneşköy: hospitality, generosity and trust building among villagers and city people.

The End of Güneşköy

Sadly, very soon, Güneşköy, our Sunvillage, will be destroyed. A high-speed train connecting Ankara with the north-east will cut through our land. According to the legal situation, there is nothing we can do. We will receive some money as compensation, but nothing can compensate for the loss — all the work, the love and the trust that grew with the villagers. The same will happen to our neighbours, an elderly couple: they will lose everything they worked for throughout their entire lives.

We refuse to lose hope. Today, people from the sustainability movement are meeting everywhere in the country. Ankara is full of beautiful, energetic meetings, Istanbul as well. From these grow 'local parliaments' which come together and discuss collective action. Lots of things are happening in Turkey and in many places. We continue to create positive examples.

Inci runs a course on Sustainable Living and Green Chemistry at the university. Some of our neighbours and students occupied a piece of land in two different locations belonging to the local government, starting city farms in front of the municipality. The municipality even helped to build a fence and supplied water!

We raised the question: Is it possible to feed Ankara from the region? One of the Mayors from the opposition party in Ankara understands that big cities should have a larger belt of villages around them for food security. The Mayor has started a village-urban initiative, resulting in a big market in downtown Ankara, with villagers bringing farm life to Ankara: straw bales in the streets, seed exchange markets and information about organic agriculture.

What's our next project? We are considering a new centre for local seed management. Our vision is to found a research institute in a village, which is used and run by villagers, not by companies. We trust that this project will bring hope and energy for the young, the women and all of us!

Keyword for Solution Library:

CSA Farming 1 — setting up direct relationships between growers and consumers of agricultural products
solution.ecovillage.org

63

Building a Healing Biotope

Tamera / Portugal

Healing Biotope 1 at Tamera (with 150 coworkers) consists of a solar village, water retention landscape, an educational peace centre, a love school, a political ashram and much more. Its aim is to develop a holistic model of a peace culture. Founded in 1995 by Dieter Duhm and Sabine Lichtenfels, it arose from a prior community that was established in 1978 in Germany. Vera Kleinhammes, daughter of the founding couple, is now part of the management team.

Vera Kleinhammes

Vera Kleinhammes

Tamera was sung into existence by the compassionate hearts of the founders. After their involvement in the protests against the war in Vietnam, and in the peace movement in general, they came to the conclusion that war is an external expression of humanity's internal landscape of pain. The construction of a sustainable peace culture not only requires ecologically and technologically sound structures, but also an inner process of healing. The development of the community was a strategic response to violence. The founders wanted to create a space for co-existence that generates trust amongst humans and all living beings.

Growing up in Community

As a child I lived in a wholesome world. Grownups around me responded to me and all my questions with respect. As children, we were raised at the centre of community life: we could watch and help out with all the work; relate to all the people; we were friends with the trees in the forest and the garden. Besides my parents, I could also choose other adults as mentors and guardians. Every night, the community gathered in the library, and as children we would fall asleep blissfully while the adults were involved in in-depth conversations about the state of the world.

I was only four when I became consciously aware of the fact that there are wars in our world. I could not understand why, and a part of me still does not understand. I was thrown out of the paradise of childhood into the mad world of adults. I desperately started searching for answers and told my mother that we had to speak to all those involved in wars and then they would stop. Soon I realised that there were too many people, and instead I suggested that we should talk to God as he can talk to all of them at the same time. Today, I have similar discussions with my son. A child's logic can be an important source of inspiration for solutions. The world is influenced by unseen forces — for example, I believe that we co-create morphogenetic fields — which have great potential for the global healing of humanity. The political theory that my father drafted builds on this, and demonstrates why small communities of people can, indeed, initiate great change.

At the age of 14, I made the conscious choice to move to Tamera. My parents already lived there whilst I went to school in Germany and lived in the ZEGG community. Up until this point I had lived in community because I was born into it. Now, I started to become interested in what my parents and so many other people were trying to realise. It dawned on me that this was my path, too!

Photo: Simon du Vinage

The Water Retention Landscape of Tamera has turned a site that was threatened by desertification into a fertile and rich permaculture ground.

Political Compassion and the Global Campus

"There can be no island of happiness in a world of suffering", says the German singer, Konstantin Wecker. This is why we search, not only for personal solutions, but also for solutions that support those in areas of crisis. We gather knowledge from experts across the globe and integrate their insights into a holistic model of a peace culture.

Our water retention landscape and permaculture practices offer solutions for landscape healing and sustainable food production in regions that are threatened by desertification. The Test Field of the **Solar Village** is off the grid, with a Scheffler mirror, biogas plant and solar collectors for everyday living. The **Escola de Esperanza** — School of Hope — is an international school, in the process of legalisation, and will also be available for local children. A stone circle and pilgrimage paths form a landscape shrine to communicate with the earth. With the **Global Campus** and the **Terra Nova School**, Tamera is connecting to a worldwide network of peace projects. Our working partnership and membership in the Global Ecovillage Network gives us strength and inspiration in recognising and supporting one another on the same quest.

Tamera has proven to be a vitalising factor for its region in southern Portugal. Rural exodus and desertification have taken their toll here, and our experience can be very useful for the revitalisation of villages, and even entire regions. I love the vision of relatively autonomous bioregions, where the youth can find sensible education and jobs, and all the inhabitants celebrate the abundance of their land, in the sense of water quality, food quality, and a neighbourhood that is alive.

Inner and Outer Community Building

The most important thing for us is building deep trust within community. Our leading example is a healing biotope: a system in which, through interplay with others, every being finds its place and, through that, initiates self-healing. The community is divided into subgroups: the autonomy group, the political ashram, school group, guest and education group and more. Within these groups, and in the community as a whole, we come together several times during the week to study and share deeply. We have three basic ethical rules: truth, mutual support and responsible participation.

It requires daily practice to live up to these ethics and to strengthen and build up a true coexistence: a space in which we sincerely reconnect with each other. Emotions such as anger are not evil or destructive at their source. It is only through suppression and judgement that these emotions become dangerous. The ability to open up in a circle of trust carries with it immense healing possibilities. Where there is consciousness, war cannot prevail. It is like water: if you don't allow it to flow, but keep damming it up, it is inevitable that, at some point, the dam will burst. It is not the water that is violent, but rather the way it is being treated. Similarly, if the human heart has been disowned for centuries, then it will become deceitful and evil. Those who have the experience of being loved for who they are without needing to wear masks, discover a completely different side of themselves.

Photo: Simon du Vinage

67

Forum is a way to communicate in large group and create transparency and trust.

The Love School

Our Peace work also embraces the interpersonal crisis area of partnership, love and sexuality. The reconciliation between man and woman is an underlying historic need. So much happiness in life depends on the perspective of love. At the core most people feel unloved. Out of fear they start to cling to the other, and like sand, their love ends up running through their fingers. In the end, many couples break up: the exact opposite of what was intended! For us, free love means taking responsibility for love. We aim to develop in such a way that we are loyal to our love and those we love, even at those painful times when our own wounds are touched. Once all people accept and love themselves, they can stop pretending to be something they are not, and men and women can trust each other again.

In many countries there are women who are being abused, or punished and ostracised for their sexual activity. Deep peace work is required so that women can express themselves fearlessly. Sexuality in old age is another topic that requires healing and education. The Love School of Tamera looks at these and many other questions. Sexuality is free if it can create trust. Love can find endurance if lovers can be safe enough to be truthful.

The Parent School forms part of the Love School, and caters for people who would like to become parents. It addresses practical questions around pregnancy, birth, and raising children, and also teaches how to consciously and knowledgeably accompany the process of conception, pregnancy and birth. Our two midwives assist homebirths throughout Portugal.

Management Structure

This is a topic that challenges us continuously. It requires trust and maturity to build true democracy. I believe this requires people with great leadership qualities: with participatory skills, capacity for teamwork and a good capacity for overview. A group leader is ready to receive feedback from others and brings the courage to dare something new so that the old patterns don't simply repeat themselves. We work in-depth with questions like: What is leadership without guru connotations? How does one help true skills of responsibility and passion to flourish amongst community members? (The tendency to offload responsibility leads to an overload within the management team.) How do we transition to new generations of management without losing depth, while simultaneously enabling the new generation to develop their unique qualities and strengths?

Mistakes and Difficulties

One main difficulty we face, in my opinion, is to participate as peace workers in a world where so much needs to be done, and at the same time avoid turning into workaholics. This is relevant both personally and for the community. How can we manage everything that needs to be done while still finding enough time to savour and celebrate life? At first the founders had assumed that after three years of social experimentation they would have set up the foundations for a new way of living together. They thought that after these years, they would be able to completely dedicate themselves to external peace work. However, there are some topics that keep resurfacing on new levels and in different ways. Often it is hard to accept that the madness of the world still holds so much power over us, despite the experience of healing, trust and solidarity.

A further challenge is our external development: a few years ago, we were prohibited from continuing further construction on our site. According to the nature protection policy, our land has exhausted its construction capacity. In reality, this means that many people have to live in caravans: which is not our ideal picture of an ecological communal life. We want to grow and show that it is possible to establish villages in such a way that they do not disturb nature, but rather support it. Already, through our work, biodiversity, reforestation and soil fertility has considerably increased. The authorities are helping us take appropriate legal steps, which also involve developing a master plan for our ecovillage for the next 15 years — maybe an exemplary process for the ecovillage movement.

The history of our project entails a very painful difficulty that we, hopefully, have left behind us now: namely, that the press or the church accused us of being a sect, and Dieter Duhm was labelled a guru. They assumed the most absurd crimes that, in reality, had never happened. This had a great impact on the development of the project. But I guess this belongs to the friction that any new development may experience, and for us it was a valuable lesson.

I am proud of the variety, the deep humanity, and the solidarity that our community has to offer. I also love the complexity with which we work. Everything is happening out of our care for the world and our love for life.

www.tamera.org

Keywords for Solution Library:

Forum — building trust and transparency in groups

Water Retention Landscape — storing rainwater using natural materials and the contours of the landscape to counteract desertification

Parents' School — preparing the ground for happy children

solution.ecovillage.org

69

Alternative in the Mainstream

Ecovillage Sieben Linden / Germany

The inhabitants of Ecovillage Sieben Linden form a diverse community.

The ecovillage Siebenlinden is a community project with around 140 inhabitants in Sachsen Anhalt, former Eastern Germany. Since 1997, the community has been realising a sustainable living style within the social, cultural, economic and ecological dimensions. Dieter Halbach, one of the founders, wrote this report.

Dieter Halbach

Dieter Halbach

The son of a single mother, I grew up at the beginning of the 50s in West Berlin, in a high-rise building devoid of nature. If the doorbell rang at all, it was to our great surprise. My yearning for community grew out of this isolation.

During the anti-nuclear protests, we founded the Republik Freies Wendtland, a living camp for protesters. From that moment on, I knew that I wanted to establish a village that could not be evicted by the police.

For 10 years I attempted living in a beautiful, yet small and isolated community in Italy, with all its shadow sides. I went through the painful experience of separating from my wife, and her leaving with our daughter. This experience clarified my longing to create a bigger community in which children can find a safe haven beyond the behaviour of their parents. I am now happy that my second daughter, despite another separation, is growing up in a protected ecovillage, while my friendship with her mother has healed over time.

It took 7 years, from 1990 to 1997 to actually establish the ecovillage. During this time, there were three points of support. First, the already existing network of community projects in the German speaking arena, and the experience they brought. Secondly, the UN Conference in 1992 in Rio that set goals for social and ecological sustainability. Lastly, the social climate in former East Germany: after the fall of the Berlin Wall in 1989, socialism broke down, but not the longing for community.

In 1990, we organised a community festival with 1,000 people. Some people from the East who felt a longing for real community met with existing communities from the West. Our ecovillage initiative had its first public appearance. The original dream was for a 100% self-sufficient ecovillage of 300 inhabitants. Over time, we softened our goals to include: self-sufficiency within the region, not the community; global networking; and human inner work and spirituality.

From the outset I was adamant that human topics would need to take centre stage. Self-reflection and transparent communication are elixirs for communities. To survive, a group needs a trustworthy human centre.

We established a cooperative and searched for a piece of land and an existing village that would take us in and set up a building plan with us. In Europe such a plan was unheard of!

71

By 1993 we were still searching. We settled into the village Gross Chueden and started setting up the first project centre with a school, a workshop, seminar rooms and a small community. The development of this centre was challenging and cost us a lot of energy. Children and adults were overexerted. After 3 years, people were tired and had lost their enthusiasm for the larger idea of an ecovillage. In this time of uncertainty, a miracle took place that enabled us to manifest our original dream — the German Foundation for the Environment, a government institution, was running the TATorte (ActionHubs) Competition. An official report showed that the 'blooming landscapes' promised by Chancellor Kohl to transform the communist wastelands, had not only not started flowering, but had never materialised. The TATorte Competition was created precisely to help create blooming, thriving regions. For this they identified 5 projects annually that show best practices and solutions in the dimensions of ecology, economy and culture.

Starting Afresh

In 1996 our initiative won this prize. Attached were a movie, an exhibition and a book about us. With this publicity, we were revived into action and hosted a one-month long exhibition at the administrative district office. We were present every day and invited mayors. We were carriers of hope and no longer ready to quit. The district administrator gave a (slightly forced) speech on the importance of going for one's dreams.

We had passed through the eye of the needle and started afresh. In 1997, we found a dilapidated farm in Poppau adjacent to an existing village. The community of Poppau requested planning approval for a second village to be established next to theirs. I very much appreciated and honoured the community for taking the risk and accepting a foreign body of 300 people into their neigbourhood. From the beginning we had interesting relations between the existing villagers and the ecovillagers: for both parties it was important that they could live their lives without interference as two interrelated but independent organisms living in good accord.

By going ahead with purchasing the dilapidated farm, we took a risk. If planning approval was declined we would not be able to build a village. Our building plan was very different — the usual trend was for bigger town centres to be built in rural areas. We had to provide evidence that we were a model project that would regenerate ecosystems and attract people into the area. Everything had to be considered: the complete infrastructure, energy supply and water cycle. Luckily we were well supported by the provincial government, as the Environmental Minister Heidrun Heidecke was a good friend of ours. However, we needed each of the government authorities to give their approval.

During this vulnerable time, a local newspaper accused us of being a sect. Such an unfounded accusation can serve as a death sentence for any intentional community. Through the Come Together Network (a community network) we were collaborating with the community 'ZEGG', which had experienced a similar, equally unfounded, accusation. A pastor declared that we were abusing children. We all know how difficult it is to contradict and especially, clear the air, after accusations of this kind.

Yet thanks to our contact with the faction leader of the Green Party, Pastor Jochen Tschiche, we contacted the church leadership and convinced them to publically retract every accusation against us and ZEGG. I picked up the representative from the Evangelic Church and drove him to the village meeting, where he was supposed to acquit us. In the car, he changed his terms and said we had to exclude ZEGG from the Come Together Network. I asked him whether there was any evidence against ZEGG, and he replied there wasn't any. So I responded that acting on his request would not correspond to my Christian values of loving my neighbour, and that I could not possibly throw an innocent fellow brother or sister out of the boat in order for the boat to reach the shore more easily.

Despite my efforts, he repeated the accusations against us at the meeting. We were in despair. Suddenly, a young pregnant woman from Poppau stood up and asked him directly: 'So, do you believe that these ecovillagers pose a threat to children or not?' He said, 'No'. And so we turned a new page. We invited the village for coffee, cake and volleyball for the following Sunday at 2pm.

73

Ecovillage Sieben Linden´s long path to becoming
officially acknowledged was worth it.

A Long-Standing Bond

On that day we prepared everything in excitement. 2pm arrived and we still waited. The ecovillage and Poppau village are connected by a long straight road. Finally, we saw around 100 people coming our way. They were holding hands, grandparents, children, all villagers, walking together. Remembering that moment gives me goose bumps to this day.

We celebrated together and I asked them: "What about the accusations?" Their reply was: "Do you think we believe everything that is printed in newspapers?" This was a great turning point. A tie of mutual trust was formed that survives today. If a conflict arises, we come together to solve it. For instance, when the car tyres on hunters' vehicles were slashed close to the ecovillage, instead of calling the police, they first asked us whether we might know who had done this. We responded by saying that we would enquire after it. A meeting of hunters and animal rights activists took place and solved the issue. Every 1st of May we celebrate together in Poppau whilst playing volleyball and enjoying cake — for me this is a peace celebration.

To realise the building plan we started a dialogue process that reached as far as the state government. They finally confirmed with us that we were a pilot project that was implementing ecological and social sustainability. In 1998, we celebrated the opening, although we still did not have the approval of the building plans. The mayor of Poppau asked: "What are you celebrating?" and I replied: "We are celebrating the principle of hope!" During this very celebration the news arrived from the planning office: the building plan had been approved. That was a celebration indeed! We had overcome many hurdles, and accepted the presence of uncertainty. We succeeded because we had support from the people from the village, the authorities, the state government and the TATorte competition. It was a magical support that reached far beyond what we as a community could have achieved alone.

Today we are a bit closer to the mainstream. Our ecovillage is recognised and used by the wider community. Politicians from all parties come with questions, from the conservative party's demographic working group that wants to understand why we are the only village that grows in the area, to the more left-wing parties, who are interested in methods of peaceful communication. That is the beauty of our ecovillage, the diversity and complexity that we embrace, from the forest kindergarten to care of the elderly, from decentralised energy and sewage systems to innovative decision-making processes. On all levels, we are involved in topics of current social interest. Since we established ourselves the press has had only positive reports about us.

Inevitably there are shadow sides. The ecovillage is located in a structurally weak region. There is no flowering cultural centre around us. We tend to stew in our own soup too much. It takes a lot of strength to find the right decisions. A professionalisation, in a positive sense, is still in its initial stages. This is similar to other communities. We all ask how to reach the next steps in such a way that we are not overexerted and have more air to breathe, more space for unfolding individuality, more space for innovation and entrepreneurship.

For me as a visionary, our processes take too long. At times there is too much personal sensitivity. This is one reason why, after 25 years, I have decided to leave. But it is not a dramatic "I am leaving you". Establishing and building the ecovillage made sense and still makes sense. I found many companions along the way, including people from sectors and organisations where I would have least expected to find support. For these people, it took courage to speak out for us. They took a risk. It is always important that we change our glasses regularly to allow recognition: there are companions on the path from all sectors in wider society and their numbers are increasing day by day.

www.siebenlinden.de

Keywords for Solution Library:
Strawbale Building 1 — using strawbales as the perfect combination of natural bricks and insulation
Wild Salad Business — building social enterprise while enriching ecosystems
Compost Toilets 1 — reducing water pollution while producing natural fertilizer for reforestation
solution.ecovillage.org

AFRICA

The Miracle in the Desert

Sekem / Egypt

Led by a vision to promote sustainable development of the individual, society and the Earth, Dr. Ibrahim Abouleish began to cultivate the hot, arid sandy ground of Egypt. Here he started a community to explore new approaches to economy, science, culture and societal life. He named this initiative Sekem — the ancient Egyptian hieroglyph for 'vitality'. Today, 2000 people are involved in the community structures of Sekem. Dr. Abouleish has received many awards for his achievements, including the 'Right Livelihood Award', and an honorary doctorate from Graz University.

Dr. Ibrahim Abouleish

Dr. Ibrahim Abouleish
Deep Vision

I carry a vision deep within myself: in the midst of sand and desert, I see myself standing at a well, drawing water. Carefully I plant trees, herbs and flowers and wet their roots with the precious drops. The cool well water attracts humans and animals to refresh and quicken themselves. Trees give shade, the land turns green, fragrant flowers bloom, insects, birds and butterflies show their devotion to God, the creator, as if they were citing the first Surah of the Koran.

The beginning, 1977: the land, which stretched out in the desert fallow and empty towards the horizon, was gently hilly. I liked the fact that it was not as flat as the delta. After a few more steps in the shimmering heat, a vision appeared before my inner eye: I saw the wells, plants, animals, compost heaps, houses and working people here. We would have to expend a lot of energy to cultivate such impassable, difficult surroundings and to transform this wasteland into a garden! So many jobs could be created in doing so, and so many people would have the chance to educate themselves while creating something healing for the landscape!

After buying the land in the desert north of Cairo, a period of intense planning began. From the very beginning, Sekem was to be a model for sustainable development, where farming, making products and services, business, education, cultural and social development are part of an holistic approach. We have also been working on the transformation of the desert into fertile land; restoring and maintaining a healthy soil and biodiversity in nature by applying biodynamic agricultural methods.

Water is a key factor in the desert. Right from the beginning, we dug five wells on the farm, with a depth of 100-110 metres. Even before the first water was pumped up from the depths, I had been thinking a lot about its distribution through an irrigation network. How should we channel the water so that it could reach the plants and animals? You need a clever plan to irrigate effectively. Canals have to be built and pipes laid. Nowadays Sekem is crisscrossed by a huge underground irrigation system

Organic Agriculture has become the basis for our successful cultivation.

"Every morning all co-workers
come together in a circle.

Sekem's own farms and those of our suppliers are cultivated according to the principles of biodynamic farming. The continuous enhancement of soil fertility has been achieved through compost prepared from organic materials. To ensure the quality and purity of the crops, healthy organic seeds and seedlings are produced on-site at the Sekem main farm. Modern grafting techniques result in increased productivity of seedlings, high resilience against soil diseases, and better adaptation to an extreme climate. Other recent innovations include the breeding of predators for natural pest control and the application of Effective Microorganisms in wastewater purification. Modern laboratories monitor the quality and purity of soil, the compost and harvested produce.

Sekem's Expansion

Egypt has lost much of its knowledge of traditional medicine since the pharmaceutical industry entered the market. Sekem introduced herbal teas in the country and started a huge awareness campaign 25 years ago. Today Sekem is the market leader in herbal teas and in the production of phytopharmaceuticals. Our development of biodynamic cultivation methods for cotton in 1992 was also revolutionary for Egypt. Convincing field trials led to a change in government policy which ended the aerial spraying of 35,000 tons of pesticides per year.

In recent years, new areas of desert land have been acquired and transformed into fertile soils through Sekem's organic cultivation. In Egypt and worldwide, both additional fertile land and its sustainable cultivation will be crucial to ensuring future food security.

79

Approximately 850 farmers from all over Egypt are now members of the Egyptian Biodynamic Association, which we established. The Association advises and instructs the farmers and works to promote biodynamic agriculture in Egypt based on scientific methods. Once a month, all farmers working together with Sekem meet. It is very impressive when, at each meeting, around two hundred tall, strong men with huge beards wearing long galabeyas stand up and express, often with tears in their eyes, how much they feel supported by Sekem. Their simple words, which come straight from their hearts, show that they see an ideal of economic life realised, based on brotherliness rather than competition and egoism.

Today, Sekem runs a variety of successful companies, producing organic foods, spices, tea, textiles from organic cotton, and herbal medicines for local and international markets. A fairly organised supply chain — from farmers to final consumers, based on trust, transparency, fair pricing and contracts — defines the 'Economy of Love' that Sekem stands for. An Economy of Love ensures that everyone in the supply chain is getting a fair part of the added value, enough to develop themselves, enough to satisfy one's own needs and the needs of one's family and one's community, while regenerating one's natural environments. The Economy of Love is very similar to 'Fair Trade'.

The desert has turned green through application of organic agriculture.

Web of Organs

The Sekem community is built on equality and respect for the dignity of every individual. For all employees in Sekem's companies and institutions, from farmers to managers, the working day starts by meeting in a circle: a symbol for equality and unity of the shared vision.

The vibrant network of the Sekem community needs functioning organs, as in every living organism: it needs social institutions that secure rights and claim responsibility, organisations which set rules to guarantee equality and to support the main goal of developing the dignity and full potential of every member of the community.

In Sekem, economic growth and the promotion of cultural impulses go hand in hand. Profits made from fair economic trade are invested in cultural and social institutions. Through continuous training and art courses, employees have the possibility of improving their skills and unfolding their inner potential. In 1989, the Sekem School opened its doors to hundreds of children from local communities. In the Sekem Kindergarten, children can play creatively. Sekem Elementary School promotes learning and practical skills, which are then further extended into the Secondary School, or the Vocational Training Centre. In 2012 Heliopolis University was founded to support further professional development.

Sekem's holistic development work includes compassionate care of children and adults with special needs, and their integration into a suitable work environment. For children whose social circumstances led them to drop-out of school, the Chamomile Children's Programme offers basic education followed by vocational training. They work part-time on the farm, carrying out light tasks such as harvesting chamomile blossoms enabling them to support their families.

In cooperation with national and international partner organisations, Heliopolis University conducts research in the fields of art, medicine, pharmacy, organic agriculture, economics, social sciences and technology. Interdisciplinary research teams work to improve agricultural cultivation methods, to develop new products for the Sekem companies or to adapt green technologies to the local context.

An ecologically sustainable community needs a healthy environment and healthy members. The Sekem Medical Centre provides medical care for approximately 40,000 people from the surrounding areas. Medical specialists use modern techniques of diagnosis and therapy and prescribe natural pharmaceuticals.

Helmy Abouleish

We were all so engulfed in work that the Egyptian revolution of 2011 took us by surprise. Through false accusations, Helmy Abouleish, my son, ended up in investigative custody. He recalls the inner stillness that spread in him after he heard. For 100 days, he lived without a telephone or appointments. He found this period to be a big chance for personal new beginnings.

In the end, he was acquitted and, since then, has focused back on the tasks in Sekem. But these difficult personal challenges, in a time of national crisis, have spurred a great advancement, both personally and for Sekem as a whole. In the three years since the revolution, two thirds of all businesses in Egypt collapsed. Sekem prevailed. That is the miracle of our times.

I see that in the meanwhile, my original vision of sustainable development has spread to the national level. Today the Egyptian government has implemented land resettlement projects in current desert areas. Villages are emerging so that people can found new communities. The experience of the Sekem pedagogy is having an increasing influence on the student curriculum and teacher education within our society.

I always stand up and appeal for the formation of authentic communities. We humans are not efficient alone. This would be an illusion. Sekem arose out of encounters of earthliness and soulfulness, and became something new. We are proving that, by creating sustainability in all dimensions, and by investing in the education of our coworkers, we can build thriving economies.

So I feel confident in saying: without Sekem there would be something missing from this world.

www.sekem.com

Keywords for Solution Library:

Herbal Teas — providing alternatives to pharmaceutical medicines
Grafting — combining different plant species in order to lessen the use of herbicides
solution.ecovillage.org

African Intellectuals Back to their Roots

Natoun / Togo

Tiyeda Abalah from Togo returned to the village of Baga together with her husband Seda after completing her literature studies in France. Today she stands amidst a flowering women's initiative, an organic school for agriculture and economy, several reforestation and water projects and a village bank that allows the village to retain its wealth. Since 2009 ecovillage Natoun has become an urgently relevant example of dignified rural living amidst the rural exodus that brings 17 million Africans across the continent into urban slums each year.

Tiyeda Abalah

Tiyeda Abalah

True African independence can only take hold once the intellectuals of the continent re-connect with their roots. It requires academics to leave their well-paid city jobs and return to their home villages, where they can share their knowledge and improve local circumstances. My husband and I arrived into the dying arms of his home village Baga at the outskirts of the desert. Every year the soil brought forth less harvest. Men left the village and left behind women with no voice. Today, this has fundamentally changed. Women have learnt to take their fate into their own hands. Their voices now help the village to blossom.

Background Story

I learnt in my childhood how important the sovereignty of women is while witnessing my mother's competitive struggle with the second wife. I did everything to win the liking of my father´s second wife hoping she would not wish to poison me when my mother was away. One strategy I evolved was that of storytelling. This assisted me later in receiving education, and learning English in Ghana. There I met Seda who became my husband, and later I followed him to France. I studied black American literature in Paris while he studied International Law in Toulouse.

We got married and had two children. He attained a PhD but this did not increase his happiness. Once we moved back to Togo, he was still unhappy — he was working in an office and yearned to touch the earth again. The many years in France had awakened his homesickness and his desire to show his family and neighbours that an honourable and wealthy way of living is possible on rural land.

Baga

But Baga was not the village he remembered from his childhood. Land which once brought forth rich harvests now lay deserted and barren. Forests and rivers had disappeared, homesteads fallen into ruins. It appeared that the desert was swallowing the village and anybody who wanted to achieve something in life had to move to the city. Initially we were not welcomed in the village. Our unusual decision to come home caused uneasy feelings: people preferred to see us in the city, feeling proud of us there. However, we stayed true to our path and acquired an extremely poor piece of land. This was exactly what we wanted, in order to show how to re-green the desert and co-create abundance and fulfillment.

At first we were alone and worked hard to cultivate the land. We ploughed the land with oxen, sowed grain, planted gardens with fruit trees and set up trenches for irrigation. We made use of cow and goats' dung and mulched. We re-introduced organic farming methods into an area where fertilisers and monoculture had been forcefully introduced and had spread for decades.

It was hard and strenuous work, and the women in the neighbourhood could not bear to watch the 'Doctor' much longer and soon joined in to help. With this a women's initiative was established that is sustained until today. African women on the land benefit most from any improvements as poverty due to climate change hits them first. Most men think that children are the affair of women only. Often, they cannot handle poverty, hunger and crying children and leave their families behind. This leaves women alone with the task of feeding children and themselves.

We have transferred knowledge to lighten their load. We have also learned a lot from them. They teach us their rituals, dances and songs that have been part of their working day for a very long time. These are the cultural roots of this land. It was vital not to throw out local wisdom and culture with modernisation, but rather allow both influences to develop a sustaining symbiotic relationship. These are our roots and if we cut them (like colonisation did), then we lose our self-worth and turn into puppets easily ruled by destructive powers.

Education

We opened a school and employed teachers in organic farming, accounting and management. Women, men and youth from the surrounding area have received their training here. The curriculum was created in a participatory way which involved the villagers. The students learn 70% practical and 30% theory. In their final year they receive an assignment to go back to their families and negotiate for a piece of land they can manage and produce from. If they succeed, they receive the task of advising and assisting their neighbours. This ensures that graduates stay on the land and assist in resuscitating villages around them.

Initially the government of Togo was very sceptical of us. However, it has now adopted our methods and is in the process of implementing them nationally. Since 2009 we have left most of the running of the school and the centre to the next generation and started focusing our energies on Ecovillage Natoun. The houses at Natoun are built traditionally with local building materials such as adobe, earth and grass. One building acts as a guesthouse for city dwellers, students and visitors from the network. Two more serve as a workshop and a preservation and storage room for seeds and harvested products.

85

Group-strength

Water remains a key topic here in Togo and in the rest of Africa. In Baga, the dry season lasts around seven months. Without appropriate decentralised water management these are wasted months in which nothing can grow. There is enough rain during the rainy seasons that can be retained and harvested, and we have already built the first three retention ponds — fruit trees around them grow well.

The women that work with us also use their knowledge at home, success then brings them self-esteem. In the early days the village meetings consisted of speaking men and listening women. Although they were not prohibited from speaking, women never felt their voice worthy of being heard outside their home. One day, the men were talking about the desert and how there was nothing that could be done to stop it spreading, similar to the great Nothing from 'The NeverEnding Story' that devours everything.

Photo: Hans-Martin Kaup

Learning and working with the ecovillage initiative created joy and self-confidence for the women from Baga.

This is when it happened: a woman spoke up! She explained that if bushes and trees grow on barren land, they can regenerate topsoil with the shade their leaves offer. This fertile earth can allow millet to grow again. Stunned silence followed her words. Some men looked at her with doubt, others with curiosity. After all, the woman looked healthy and her children seemed well fed, too. One of the men started to enquire who she was, to which man she belonged and where she had heard these melodies. Her husband became proud of her and started to spend more time at home, in the field and garden. Rumours started spreading of how women were learning sensible things here. More women wanted to join the project. And so we grew.

The women in Baga worked so successfully that they could start selling produce. Then they came up against the next hurdle for disadvantaged women: the politics around pricing used by middlemen. When the grain was ripe and the women were eager to sell it, prices dropped to rock bottom. The dealers knew the women were desperate for money. If the women agreed to such a deal and thereafter showed interest in buying machinery, seeds or other things, the prices for these would sky rocket. On their own, they did not stand a chance. So, they united stand up for their rights in the village council and everywhere else. They started selling their produce directly in the market. When the mayor tried to stop this, they blockaded his office until he opened his heart.

One solution against dependence on market prices is the Village Bank that we established. The system is simple, yet effective: for a small administration fee, every inhabitant can become a member and take their money to the village bank and withdraw it at any time. This enables women to buy and sell when the prices are fair. They support one another if one requires help. This has little to do with micro credits as the women stay debt free. For instance, they use their money when the soya beans are cheap and produce soya cheese which they then sell on the market. The profit they deposit again. Or they buy nuts and oils with which they produce organic soaps. Jam, dried fruits — the list of products that the women have on offer in the surrounding markets is increasing.

Organic gardening brings economic benefit to the village while helping to prevent desertification.

Eventually the village was released from the sharp and tight claws of poverty. I believe that local change has a global effect because success is contagious. The women from Baga are wealthier and the land has become more fertile. This new story travels by word of mouth and others start copying us, 'just like the women in Natoun'. There is no reason why this method cannot spread to the entire country. An active village community with healthy traditions and knowledge about sustainable management can bring about a positive revolution! Humanity needs such examples and we are trying to set them.

www.thedancingforest.com

Keywords for Solution Library:

Farmers Bank — strengthening local economies
Agricultural School — educating future generations in organic farming

solution.ecovillage.org

Genius in the Townships

OTEPIC / Kenya

Shabby looking huts, ragged children, narrow alleyways flooded
with sewage, and garbage: this is the reality of Mitume, Kitale in the
northwestern part of Kenya. Lack of prospects and environmental
destruction are part of the colonial inheritance. Africa and its people are
in a process of reclaiming their traditions, their sense of self-worth and
community, and their rights to land.

Philip Odhiambo Munyasia, 31, was one of the kids that grew up in the
streets of Kitale. Today, he mobilises youth and women to help themselves
through organic food production, reforestation, sustainable water and
renewable energy solutions. Conflict resolution for gang and tribal rivalries
form an important part of building a viable future. The radiant sunflowers
at the very centre of the township reflect hope. Philip's vision comprises an
international permaculture training centre and ecovillage. The first huts,
built from recycled materials and clay on a dedicated piece of land, have
been realised.

Photo: Leila Dregger

Philip Munyasia

Philip Munyasia

My Background

I am the youngest of eight brothers. As a child, I experienced what it means to collect firewood on an empty stomach and what it feels like not to have clean drinking water. The daily pressures of accumulating bare necessities, of survival under challenging circumstances led to tensions and conflicts amongst the different ethnic groups. Violence, drug abuse and criminal activities thrived. Since I was a little boy, I have dreamt of changing this situation.

The region of Kitale is blessed with two rainy seasons, fertile soil and a mild climate. Yet this abundance does not benefit the population. Most Kenyans have access to very little or no land. The land had been in the care of the local people for centuries — but it was appropriated by the government and sold to foreigners from countries such as China, Saudi Arabia, India and Europe. We are well acquainted with international maize and rose companies producing for an international market, and it is due to similarly intensive agriculture over the past decades that the soil suffers from salination. The groundwater has been polluted, rivers have dried out, the forests have been cut down and the desert is spreading.

Displaced refugees from a variety of ethnic backgrounds have arrived in Mitume. People no longer believe that anything good can grow from this place. By European standards, it is a slum. We have no electricity and live with big families in small shacks. We have no flushing toilets or running water and there is a strong stench of plastic and charcoal, used by women for cooking.

The children go to school without breakfast. When they come home for lunch, and see smoke rising from their home, they know there will be food. If not, they go back to school on an empty stomach and concentration is made impossible. The teachers beat those of them who made mistakes.

When I was small, my mother borrowed money to grow corn. To be sure not to make mistakes, she asked for advice from an agricultural expert. He advised her to use a specific chemical. It was a disaster. All of the plants died. The garden was lost. I was only five years old, but I will never forget my mother's crying.

Then a miracle happened. A Catholic priest made it possible for me to go to high school and even college. I remembered my dream. I started teaching women and smallholder farmers how to grow food organically. I received a bursary to go to the USA for six months to study permaculture. To be able to apply for my visa and passport, I needed money and so my mother sold her goats and sheep. Once I was in the USA, I studied very hard and only ate what the land offered. I therefore managed to save up all my pocket money. Out of five Kenyans who were offered this bursary, I was the only one to return home. When I returned, my friends asked me for money, thinking that now I was rich. It was very difficult to say no to them, but I had other plans for the money.

Establishing Ground

I bought a portion of land in the middle of Mitume as the first demonstration garden and pilot project. Here we showed the people how one can use the small available pieces of land in slums to plant food. When people witnessed the first raised beds we created, they thought they were graves and called us insane. As time passed people became curious at the abundant growth of food, and were eager to join. The planting methods in permaculture are similar to those of traditional Kenyan food farming: planted in mixed cultures and communities, the big plants support the small ones, and the earth is always covered.

In 2008, I established OTEPIC — a community-empowered self-help organisation. We offer regular trainings to smallholder farmers and organise women's groups on family planning, Aids and domestic violence. Furthermore, we organise tree planting projects, seed exchanges, clean-up campaigns and peace activities such as football matches between the different ethnic tribes and gangs. One youth group uses our space for theatre and dance training. Creativity is important. If it isn't fun, it's not worth it.

In the meantime, I was able to travel to Europe occasionally, which amongst many other things also allowed me to secure funds for our organisation. In 2012, we were able to extend our project on a second demonstration plot. It boasts a workshop in which unemployed youth learn techniques such as building solar cookers, rocket stoves or little biogas systems, as an alternative to using firewood as cooking fuel.

Water is a central topic here in Kenya. The paths to find water are becoming longer and the water is often contaminated. The government sells water, but not every family can afford it. I received official blessing and sufficient funds to build a 72m deep water well. The water is pumped up by solar energy. Every neighbour can simply come and get water. There is always excitement at the water well: women are washing, children are collecting water, and men are chatting. They become aware what is going on at OTEPIC, for instance the new abundance sprouting as our mushroom farming takes off, not only providing a source of nourishment, but also of income.

Community

Our teams meet early every morning and set out the work plan. At lunch time we come together to eat vegetables out of our garden, cooked with biogas or the solar cooker. Street kids join us for meals. There is a computer for everyone to use, a small library and an opportunity to watch videos. The door is always open, but nothing has ever been stolen. The community protects it, knowing that this space belongs to all of us.

Photo: Phillip Munyasia

Creating hope and new perspectives for children from slums.

Children are never sent away. They are our future. We welcome them and never underestimate their potential. Parents are often astounded at the passionate concentration their children develop.

Women within Kenyan society are not encouraged to speak their mind or show any leadership qualities. Yet 80% of smallholder farmers in Kenya are women and often they are responsible for whole families. That's why we say: "When you reach out to a woman, you reach out to an entire village." The first women's initiative called Maili Saba, (7 miles from the main town of Kitale), in which I taught, now has a community garden. Speaker Nancy Oppelle says, "Nobody is hungry any more, not even at the end of the dry season and the children are healthy. The mixed cultures produce everything we need throughout the year, unlike the previous monoculture of maize. Instead of buying fertilisers we can now use our money to buy school books for the children." Besides a diversity of fruits and vegetables, they also plant sweet potatoes. These are harvested, dried, ground, and baked into sweet little breads in the community bakery. The children sell them in town.

The women of Maili Saba making sweet potato bread.

In 2013, we were able to buy 10 further hectares of land through donor funds, bringing closer the realisation of our vision of an Ecovillage and International School of Permaculture. We conducted a participatory planning workshop, supported by permaculture teacher Mugove Walter, who has been a member of the GEN-Africa council since 2012. We concluded by building our first community hut from earth bags.

The earth came from the newly dug-out pond outside the hut, which now fills up in the rainy season. This pond is the starting point of a water landscape retention area, which will consist of many ponds and swales in the future. It will serve to have enough water for irrigation, fish farming and most importantly to raise the underground water level. We are planning to build houses and ponds in tandem.

Today, we consist of a core team of twelve people. Some are youth from Kitale who have returned from the capital, Nairobi. Our team is joined on a daily basis by ten to fifty volunteers, often women, children and youth from the neighbourhood. Every single one of them comes from difficult circumstances, and knows poverty, hunger, neglect, violence and abuse intimately. In this context of social disruption, they have been in contact with alcohol, drugs and crime. They also have immeasurable strength and are willing to do anything once they see a perspective. This is why it is important for OTEPIC to bring a vision of solidarity and community.

The church also plays an important social role. In Africa, spirituality is very important. The Europeans brought us their religion. But we, as Africans, already had access to God through our direct connection with nature. This became prohibited and people either converted to Christianity or became Muslims. In many African countries, these two religions are at war today. At OTEPIC, we say that a person's religion does not matter. What matters is that together we recognise the sacredness of simple celebrations such as going into nature together and planting trees.

A true sign of leadership in Africa is engagement and communication with the people. To stand and talk alone or give orders to others is of little use here. Development and aid workers will get nowhere if they cannot acknowledge this truth. Leadership is the art of being deeply connected to the community and listening to them in order to find out what really needs to be done and then to act together.

Sometimes people tell me that I work miracles. I also work with challenges and failure; ideas evaporated, projects faded, plans had to be postponed. Yet I cannot be held back. I must look at that what has succeeded and be filled with gratitude, for only then will abundance spread.

www.otepic.org

Keywords for Solution Library:

Earthbag Houses — building cheap and simple shelters
Bread from Sweet Potatoes — creating local food sovereignty
Portable Gardens — growing food in urban environments
solution.ecovillage.org

Ubuntu — I Am Because You Are

Greening Schools / Zimbabwe, Malawi, Zambia

Mugove Walter Nyika, council member of GEN-Africa, was born in Zimbabwe, became a permaculture and ecovillage teacher, moved to Malawi and then, recently, to the Zambia. He speaks about his memories, about the abundance of nature in his childhood, how it was destroyed, and how the wounds of nature and of the mind can heal. Through his NGOs, SCOPE and RESCOPE, he works in Zimbabwe, Malawi, Kenya, Tanzania, Uganda and Zambia, greening hundreds of schools. Starting with the next generation, their teachers and parents, he sets the foundations for transitioning whole communities to ecovillages.

Photo: Simon du Vinage

Mugove Walter Nyika

The name my parents gave me is Mugove, which means 'gift'.

I grew up with my grandparents in a village 200 km south of the capital Harare, in Zimbabwe. From an early age I learned from my grandfather to plant trees, to collect seedlings and put them into the earth. There were many sacred sites where it was a taboo to cut down a tree. When I fell asleep during the day my grandmother laid me in the shade of a tree, many of which bore fruit.

When people were clearing land for farming, they always left the fruit trees standing, even if they were in the middle of the gardens. When fencing their gardens, they incorporated the existing trees into their fencing. The land was always covered either with trees, grass, leaf litter or with a large diversity of crops planted together.

Abundance

My grandmother was a small-scale organic farmer, like most African women. On her few acres she grew many different crops: millet, maize, sweet potatoes, pumpkins, cucumber, cowpeas, ground nuts, round nuts and all kind of vegetables, many of which grew as weeds, such as Cleome. She knew how to plant crops together that would support each other. I cannot remember that I or any of my friends were ever hungry as children.

As young boys we were responsible for herding the cows of the village. In the morning we walked them to the pastures. We never carried anything to eat with us. The landscape surprised us every day, from January to December, with wild harvests such as fruits and nuts. In the afternoon when the cattle rested, we hunted some small animals or caught fish in the river and roasted them to eat.

When we came home in the evening, we looked forward to rest, because we had walked 30 km or more, but we never looked forward to dinner, as we were already full. Nature always provided us with our needs. At home, and in the bush, we always drank clean spring water. The streams flowed throughout the year and they had sparkling clear water and large pools with plenty of fish and other aquatic animals.

Barren Life and Barren Land

I went to school, became a teacher and moved to Harare. I have lived and worked in various countries in Southern Africa: Malawi, Kenya, Tanzania, Uganda and Zambia. Now when I visit my village, I find that things have changed. Whether I look to the right or to the left, I only see large fields of corn, mono-crops of corn. But they are frequently not in good shape, with many being yellow from nitrogen deficiency and wilting as the soils, depleted of organic matter, no longer hold water. The landscape is bare as the trees have been cut down — they were in the way of modern agriculture. The large variety of plants and animals have gone — killed through habitat destruction as people clear land for farming, and through the widespread use of pesticides and chemical fertilisers. In Malawi, the state spends 20 percent of the national budget on the Farm Input Subsidy Programme (FISP), which buys agrochemicals for subsidised distribution to farmers.

In Zimbabwe, most of the agricultural development resources have gone into maize production which is seen as the key to food security, but this has created challenges in terms of nutrition for both the soil and the people. The rivers, streams and springs have died: where there was water flowing in my childhood, where I caught fish — I see only sand today. I can no longer show my children a natural pool of water in the river. This is what monoculture, agrochemicals and erosion have done to the land and the people.

As a Permaculture teacher I see 9 out of 10 children come to school without breakfast. Most have what we call a 0 - 0 - 1 diet: no breakfast, no lunch, only dinner. And dinner is usually a plateful of refined corn meal and a vegetable. There lies the hidden hunger: some may have plenty to eat, but only white flour, corn, wheat or rice — 7 days a week throughout the year. The situation is worse during the dry season.

Photo: Mugove Walter

After one year a barren school yard has turned into a fruit forest.

What colonialism and globalisation have done to the land is saddening. The focus on cash crops and large-scale industrial agriculture has led to an impoverishment of soils and a dependency on foreign markets. But what it did to the people is even worse. Africans have always heard: what you learnt from your ancestors is backward, primitive. We have brought you 'progress'. What keeps the average African going today — in spite of all the misery and poverty? It is the dream that one day he will have an American lifestyle: a large home with big screen TVs, fast cars, plenty to eat from the supermarket, etc. Many Africans have taken to these values, they regard only high tech and expensive things as progress and look down on anybody who applies organic approaches — because this is what their ancestors did

— and it is seen as primitive and poor. Progress has to be complicated and expensive — easy and natural solutions are regarded as backward.

Some African girls buy dangerous bleaching chemicals to remove the black melanin pigment from their skin, in order to look whiter. Today, a 'good' African woman gets up long before sunrise and starts sweeping the compound around the house. As the light comes up all villages and townships are covered in dust. The first hour in school the children sweep the ground of the school yard. This habit of sweeping, of creating 'tidiness and order', has become a big problem. Together with erosion it destroys the topsoil, and all the organic waste is piled up and burnt. It is the organic waste that we miss as fertiliser in the gardens. Today, in Africa, we burn our natural fertiliser and then buy industrial fertilisers from Europe.

Above all, many African communities now believe that they are poor. The development agencies have been coming to them with the question: what are your problems? This sticks a poverty label in the minds of the people. They have been taught to count their many problems and not to count their blessings. To me it is obvious that Africa is the richest continent. We are sitting on a goldmine. The fertility of the soil, the sunny climate, the biodiversity which is still there, the wisdom and traditions which still can be recalled, can provide us with all our needs. But we have to acknowledge this and learn to put it together in the right way.

Permaculture

In 1996, I visited the Fambidzanai Permaculture Centre close to Harare and did my Permaculture design course — and this changed my life. Permaculture brings together the elements that have been torn apart in modern life — living, teaching, growing food. Things are not seen as separate, but mixed in mutually supportive ways. They form cycles. For me, it was like coming home: permaculture fits much better to our African way of life, to the people and the land than so-called modern industrialised agriculture.

I left my job as a teacher, and today I help schools in Zimbabwe, Malawi and other African countries to change their bare and ornamental school yards into food forests. In Zimbabwe, every school has to have a minimum of four and a half acres of land. People are surprised how easy and fast the barren soil can turn into an abundant and diverse fruit forest that can feed the children. The first step is to change the habit of sweeping and cleaning out the organic matter. We start keeping it on the land and even collecting more organic waste to cover the ground. In Africa, it rots very fast and transforms into topsoil in which we can plant the seeds. Some trees in our climate can grow more than 1.5 m a year, so the children will notice the difference in a short time. There is enough rainwater: 800 mm on average in most places. But we have to take care that it does not run away without being used. We create swales — ditches along the 'keylines' — that give the water time to filter into the ground. When the soils are moist and the rainwater is harvested, the gardens have enough water throughout the year.

The most difficult thing is to un-learn bad habits and wrong thinking patterns. For example, the mindset of tidiness: soil or organic matter is not dirt, but life. People have to understand how rich they are, and then they can see that it is not much work to create a garden.

There is hope for the future. Africa has the potential to lead the world in reconnecting to the one ecosystem that we share with all other life forms. There is still a sense of community, the spirit of ubuntu, which means: 'I am because you are'. The connection to the land is still alive on the continent. I have had the joy of working with many school communities that are showing that a different world is not only possible, but that it comes with an improved quality of life.

Of the many educational experiences that I have had in my life, I have no hesitation in saying that the Permaculture Design Course (PDC) and the Ecovillage Design Education (EDE) were the two experiences that have had the most profound impact on my life. With these wonderful tools, I am working with school communities and ecovillage initiatives to co-create a better future for everyone involved. In this work, I am part of the team that is connecting African communities to the Global Ecovillage Network (GEN). I am hopeful that all is not lost for my children and the generations to come.

Keywords for Solution Library:
Swales — harvesting rainwater to replenish water tables
Turning school yards into fruit forests — educating and nourishing the next generation
solution.ecovillage.org

Responsible Tourism

Sandele Eco-Retreat / The Gambia

Sandele Eco-Retreat in Kartong is an example of responsible tourism. The lodges are built with compressed, stabilised earth blocks that use a minimum of cement and are frequently stabilised with lime. Electricity, hot water and water are provided using solar and wind power. The Lodges and the Guest Rooms have compost toilets and a constructed wetlands system that minimises the use of, and purifies, the water flowing from the toilets, showers, hand basins and rainwater. Its founders, Geri Mitchell and Maurice Phillips from England, are working hand in hand with the local community to build the project as an integral part of the village of Kartong. Kartong is in the process of officially transitioning to become an ecovillage. Since 2014, regular Ecovillage Design Education (EDE) courses have been held, where the villagers are refining their community development plans.

Photo: Leila Dregger

Geri Mitchell and Maurice Philips

Geri Mitchell

After careers in senior management in the social care world in the UK, we began to dream of our next step being something and somewhere different. Inspirations came from many sources and we finally decided The Gambia was the place where we could realise our vision of creating a different kind of tourism. After five years changing the fortunes of the Safari Garden hotel in Fajara (now handed over to local management), we settled on the Kartong region as the location for our Eco-Retreat and Learning Centre.

In the traditional manner, we sent a gift of Kola nuts to the village elders, who then invited us to a discussion. Determined to ensure that the local community would benefit, we registered the land in the village's name. Kartong was the first village to reclaim indigenous land that had been re-owned by the government for private investment. We now sub-lease the land from the village and it will revert fully to village management at the end of the 25-year lease.

Sandele's (pronounced San-day-le) name was carefully chosen. 'Sandele' is derived from two Mandinka words (the Mandinka are the majority tribe of The Gambia). 'Sine' means 'now' and 'Dehli' means 'be still'. Often when rocking her baby to sleep, a mother will whisper the words 'Sineedehleh', 'Now be still'. This is a wonderful strap line for an eco-retreat.

Sustainability

We also very deliberately set out to create an authentic E-co-Retreat — the 'E' standing for 'Environmental' with the use of sustainable energy sources, reduction of water usage (including the decision to use composting toilets) and sustainable construction methods which was a particular challenge. We wanted to use as little of the precious timber as possible because the forests need protection. Concrete, with its high environmental impact, is not really an alternative, and locally used mud blocks were not able to resist the water during the rainy season. It was because of this that we learnt a perfect building technique from Auroville: it is possible to mix earth with lime, and then by compressing the earth in the machine we imported from India the blocks become hard and waterproof, and easy to build with. We have lots of lime that we can extract from the millions of oyster shells at the river banks, and the soil that we have here at Sandele is perfect for this kind of technique. All our buildings are made of compressed, stabilised earth blocks.

The system was so successful that we started a building company to construct buildings in this style all over The Gambia.

Photo: Leila Dregger

Responsible tourism and dream holidays in the ecolodge.

Community

The 'Co' in E-co stands for 'Community' with a commitment to hire at least 70% of staff from the local village, to purchase locally where possible and donate part of the proceeds from our room revenue to the Village Development Fund. From the beginning we took every step in consultation with the elders and the Village Development Committee. In the big hotels local people have no access, unless they are employees. Many villagers everywhere in Africa try to make a living from selling jewellery and other handicraft items to tourists, and many tourists feel disturbed by the 'bumstering' while they want to relax.

In Sandele it is done differently. Vendors are not turned away at our gates, but quite the opposite, we sit with them and offer to exhibit their products in our reception and sell it for a fair price. They make a much better income out of that. Some of the producers followed our offer to work in the workshops that we created. They have become amazing messengers for their culture while the tourists admire their skilfulness.

One of the villagers, who was actually very shy, could only speak to the tourists when he was drunk. He had become rejected by his community. Through our approach this absolutely changed. By selling his products here, he has been able to pay scholarships for two of his nephews and is well-regarded in the village now.

We spent all of our savings building the lodges and the restaurant. Some of the lessons learnt along the way were rather expensive, so our savings were exhausted earlier than we hoped. Now we build rooms when we have made a good income, which is not easy at the moment. Although The Gambia has not had a single case of Ebola, nearly all tourists and yoga groups cancelled their arrangements.

We now have to pull together to be able to employ our workers throughout the year, not only in the sunny (winter) season. We are very positive that tourists will come again. Sandele is now the last place where the forest still goes down to the beach, and the Minister of Tourism has promised to protect the bay from 'mass' tourism and deforestation. It is only a pity that most tourists miss the rainy season as the bush bursts into life, it is still very sunny and the rain is not constant by any means.

Photo: Martin Funk

Maurice has introduced compressed lime blocks all over The Gambia, as a sustainable alternative to concrete.

103

EDE

In 2014, we organised an EDE course with GEN and Gaia Education. 24 young participants came from Kartong. Learning about permaculture, community governance, land use, planning and keeping cultural heritage was a life-changing experience for all of them, and most try to apply the knowledge and skills in Kartong. There is now a permaculture garden in the village, an organic bee-keeper, and a community that invests a lot in sustaining themselves by producing traditional palm oil and wine. A project to maintain the regeneration of the fish and oyster populations in the mangroves of their river has started. They have become change agents in Kartong, with a strong wish to transition it into an ecovillage.

Of course the process is not always smooth. At times power conflicts arise and some in the village are afraid that things will get out of their control.

The Gambia has a big gift to offer the world. Gambians know how to live together peacefully even with different cultures and religions. They will also learn how to integrate their traditional knowledge into sustainability strategies.

When our 25-year lease is up, we look forward to retiring to our house on the site, under the shade of a Baobab tree, and remain a part of the community.

Gilbert Jassey, a villager from Kartong

"My family sent me to our capital Banju to study law and become a lawyer. In 2011 I saw a presentation by Kosha Joubert about Ecovillages and GEN. This inspired me so deeply that I decided to go back to Kartong and stayed there. After reading a book about permaculture and after attending an EDE course in Sieben Linden, Germany, I started a permaculture demonstration garden and helped to organise the EDE course in Kartong in 2014."

104

www.sandele.com

Keywords for Solution Library:
Responsible Tourism — creating revenue streams while protecting environments
Compressed Earth Bricks — building with local resources
Compost Toilets in Islamic Regions 4 — solving cultural discomfort with sustainable solutions
solution.ecovillage.org

Where Top-Down and Bottom-Up Strategies Meet

Mbackombel, Guédé Chantier, Senegal

Worldwide, Senegal's government is the first to implement a national ecovillage programme for sustainable development. After noticing the success of the national network, GEN-Senegal, in transitioning 45 traditional villages, in August 2008 the government decided to transition every second village of the country — 14,000 in all — into an ecovillage. While this target sounds extremely ambitious, the National Agency for Ecovillages — ANEV — has already created more than 100 ecovillages. Here, we explore the village of Mbackombel as an example of the challenges and successes of implementing a bottom-up approach through a governmental agency. Also, Dr. Ousmane Pame reports on Guédé Chantier, one of the communities of GEN-Senegal.

Photo: Leila Dregger

Mbackombel is named after the huge baobab tree that forms the centre of the village. Here, the farmers try out new ways of organic gardening with mixed cultures, seed diversity and drip irrigation.

Mbackombel and ANEV, Dr. Ousmane Pame

A drive through rural Senegal reveals the challenges of this region: the West African country is threatened with desertification and a loss of biodiversity. After many years of international pressure to move away from traditional organic agriculture towards large scale agro-industrial production the soil is often left depleted. Whole areas have been deforested by goats, and by villagers in search of firewood, leaving behind single baobab trees that define the atmosphere of the landscape. At the edge of the small villages and their thatched huts, very little grows on the dusty fields. Migration into urban slums is advancing rapidly.

Mbackombel, home to 550 families, is located about 100 km from Dakar, and is one of the ANEV pilot projects. Villagers welcome visitors by singing and dancing under the majestic baobab village tree. They then lead them to the photovoltaic systems which have changed the life of this remote village significantly. Its residents now have access to streetlights and lighting in their homes. There is even a computer room in the school with solar rechargeable laptops that enable both children and adults to connect to the world via internet. Here, the global and the local meet with surprising intimacy. The villagers developed a system where all users pay a small fee for lighting. This income finances the maintenance of the system, offering work to the local youth.

Photo: Leila Dregger

Solar panels in Mbackombel have brought light to the nights.

Ecovillage Techniques

Some women present the new firewood-saving cooking techniques. Cooking is an intimate part of any culture. However, the biogas plant, fed with the manure of their livestock, and directly connected to gas cooking stoves, is not in full use. It takes time, and requires full ownership over the process for people to change their lifestyles. In contrast, the village women were directly involved in the development of the clay rocket stoves which are now used widely. They even improved on the designs that had been made by the representatives of the University of Dakar in a rare example of grassroots teaching academia. Now the wood-saving cooking stoves are built and sold in Mbackombel and form part of the economic base of the community. Various solar cookers are used to dry peanuts and to demonstrate further solar technologies.

Other ecovillage techniques implemented at Mbackombel, with greater and lesser degrees of success include: reforestation, climate-friendly farming methods in community gardens, bio-construction with compressed earth bricks, breeding local chickens, rainwater storage ponds, water-saving irrigation methods, and protection for tree plantations against the goats. These techniques have clearly improved living standards in the village and its satellite homesteads. But the question for every development project is to what extent the process is rooted in participatory processes and owned by the people in the local community. Ideally, of course, true ownership would entail being fully involved in and rightfully proud of their achievements, and in the future, to be able to define their own development schemes. ANEV tries to attain local buy-in by only working with those communities who actively apply to become part of the programme and are willing to take responsibility for all its consequences. All population groups have to agree to this — the elders, the men, the women and the youth. They also need to agree to dedicate a part of their village land to reforestation. Another condition applied is that the villagers share their new green infrastructure with surrounding villages. A certain percentage of revenue earned from these infrastructures has to be saved through a community banking system for times of crisis, as well as an initial funding for follow-up projects.

The head of ANEV, Col. Demba Ba explains his approach, "We focus on four areas: strengthening of village governance structures; local food security, including decentralised water and soil management; renewable energy; the activation of the private sector for sustainable funding."

The ecovillage activities of the government are inspired and supported by the powerful Sufi traditions in the country. Abdulaye Makthar Diop, Grand Serigne of Dakar: "The concept of ecovillage is deeply compatible with the traditional cultures of our country. In all religions the tree is seen as a brother. In Islam, if you plant a tree, it is seen as a charity. The roots of the trees are like the roots of our people."

Global Ecovillage Summit

In December 2014 a Global Ecovillage Summit took place in Dakar. 40 countries were represented at this conference, which was hosted by GEN in collaboration with the Senegalese government. It was a fascinating challenge to bridge the gap between bottom-up and top-down approaches, but also allow the tension of the gap to be felt. Clearly, there is a lot that both sides can bring to strengthen the work of the other — with the government sector helping to mainstream an ecovillage approach for sustainable development, and GEN and Gaia Education bringing to the table their rich experience around participatory design and grassroots leadership.

At a sumptuous reception, the Senegalese Prime Minister expressed his personal commitment, as well as that of his President, to promote the ecovillage concept across the African continent. The Secretary General of the Ministry of Environment shared a resolution at the closing ceremony, proclaiming the Senegalese President's full support for GEN and the values it stood for. The icing on the cake was provided by Senegalese mega music star, Youssou N'Dour, an honorary government ministerial adviser, who announced that he would be happy to serve as a Goodwill Ambassador for GEN.

The ANEV activities build on the successful work of GEN-Senegal. One of the ecovillages belonging to this network is Guédé Chantier, and its story is told by its former mayor, and current President of GEN-Africa, Dr. Ousmane Pame.

Guédé Chantier, First Eco-community of Senegal, Dr. Ousmane Pame

Guédé Chantier in the Senegal River Valley was founded in 1933 by French colonists in order to introduce irrigated agriculture to the region. In the process, the French forced many people from villages and neighbouring countries such as Mali and Mauritania to relocate to Guédé. The development of water basins for farming at Guédé was accompanied by a considerable demographic rise. Indeed, from its original 600 inhabitants (some 50 households), Guédé's population grew to nearly 7,000 people. Today, Halpulaars (the majority), Wolofs, Sarakholés, Maures and Bambara live here in harmony.

Guédé became a prosperous socioeconomic crossroads that invigorated many bordering villages. Since the 60s, many institutions have successfully supported local agricultural development by investing in the surrounding irrigated farms that have experienced more lucrative outputs as a result. Today, Guédé Chantier alternates rice production and polyculture (tomatoes, onions, corn, okra, etc. and also produces local and exotic fruits from its family orchards, as well as honey and medical plants. Until the

70s Guéde was an oasis gifted with a unique microclimate, favoured by the numerous irrigation canals that traverse it, and characterised by the greenness of its rice paddies, its community garden, and multiple family orchards.

Open talks between the Senegalese government and GEN representatives during the GEN Summit in Dakar in December 2014.

Today, Guédé is far removed from this era of abundance and carefree living: desertification is spreading rapidly, the cycle of seasons is disrupted, plant populations are suffering, animal populations have plummeted, sand storms, once rare, are more frequent and violent, heat waves reign and soar beyond all previous records. The lives of citizens, farmers, and fishermen are thrown into disarray. The difficulties for Guédé started at the beginning of the 80s, when the agricultural sector of Guédé Chantier, now largely industrialised, started to be eaten away by multiple constraints such as the high cost of inputs (seeds, fertilisers, pesticides, etc.), lack of respect for the agricultural calendar, continuous soil and water degradation, and thus weaker and weaker yields. Many farmers got into debt. The crisis is profound and multifaceted and affects all sectors of the socioeconomic livelihood of the village.

These growing difficulties pushed the population to organise reflection days: in September 2002, over three days, all layers of the population (farmers, women, youth, fishermen, students, teachers, technicians, the unemployed, the retired) took part in the creation of a document that described all of the problems, and offered strategies for solving them. In December 2007, Guédé held a general assembly and committed to the ideals of the national network of ecovillages (GENSEN), becoming the first ecovillage in the Senegal River Valley.

The concept of an eco-community integrates the social, economic, cultural and ecological perception of the world. Beyond purely ecological concerns, ecovillages are committed to preserving and promoting the science and technology of their ancestors, and fundamental cultural values like *Jokkere éndam* — the primacy of community solidarity. This happens at the same time as implementing innovative projects that are healthier and more sustainable, and adapted to the setting that is Guédé Chantier.

Now, the Association of Eco-guardians regularly organises *set-setal* (large-scale public clean-up efforts). It educates the population through theatre-plays about the dangers of plastic litter, chemical poisons in the fields, childhood malnutrition and Sexually Transmitted Infections. This means of communication is well adapted to the setting as nearly 65% of the population is illiterate. A centre of genetic resources was created to reinforce the struggle against environmental degradation while promoting the repopulation of local species. Local seeds are produced and freely distributed to associations of farmers who receive field-school lessons on composting, seed production and organic products. Senegalese and American students regularly serve as interns to these projects. It is however necessary to note that the organisation faces many financial difficulties.

The women of the community benefit from education on techniques for processing and preserving fruits and vegetables for storage and for sale at the market. The association of women has many orchards and has organised a special economic interest group. Soon, thanks to the support of the EU, the eco-community will own a multifunctional community environmental centre that will prepare the population of Guédé and the department of Podor to adapt to the threat of climate change: desertification, soil erosion, irregular patterns of precipitation, floods, etc. The Centre will hold conferences, host film screenings, expositions, and theatrical productions. It will be equipped with computer equipment to connect the community to the youth of the world, notably with the Global Ecovillage Network. Guédé Chantier, first eco-town of Senegal, is actively supported by the State of Senegal and by many other national and international partners. Today, the strongest hope of the Eco-community is to own a community radio station, and to completely transition to the development of organic agriculture. Ecovillages may be the model that helps Senegal to find its own way into the future, as it corresponds more deeply to our traditions than the Western lifestyle.

Keywords for Solution Library:
Rocket Stove — reducing the use of firewood for cooking
Cross-Sector Dialogue — preparing the ground for societal change
solution.ecovillage.org

LATIN AMERICA

A Dream of Peace, Self-sufficiency and Samba

Sao Paulo's 'Favela da Paz' / Brazil

According to the United Nations, more than half the world's population live in cities. By 2050, it will be two-thirds. As a consequence, the slums of the cities grow. Today, nearly one billion people live in slums. In Latin America alone, they make up 24% of the population. According to the Food and Agriculture Organisation of the United Nations, the city population is threatened mostly by rising food costs and scarcity of raw materials, while violence and crime are additional afflictions. The ecovillage concept refers to villages and communities as human-scale settlements in both rural areas and urban neighbourhoods. Slums can become more sustainable and safer places as people start to feel empowered and gain a voice in society, consume fewer resources, and learn how to produce some of their food and energy. The ecovillage movement has some examples:

Jardim Angela, with its 800,000 inhabitants, was ranked by the UNO as one of the most brutal neighbourhoods in the world in the 90s. Residents living in the official city are hardly aware of this world, except that it is considered dangerous. What they do not know is that, in contrast to the anonymous city centres, here in the favela people know each other and help each other out whenever they can. The 'Favela da Paz' has grown into a model project for self-sufficiency. Claudio Miranda, 41, the man with the irresistible smile, is its part-time initiator because, in actuality, he is a musician!

Claudio Miranda

I was born and raised in this area. There is always police, drug trafficking and violence — always. It is an area where streets are full of street children and we do not let our own children into the street; where the rubbish has not been collected for 20 years because the settlement is not officially recognised; and where we never know what is worse: police or gangs.

Claudio Miranda

114

As a child, my brother and I gave concerts on tin cans. After all, there was plenty of garbage around, and real musical instruments were unattainable. The music attracted other children and so, with 13 others, I started the band Poesia Samba Soul, which still makes music today.

I do not know what would have happened to us if it were not for music. One of my best friends was shot dead during a police raid. I nearly suffered a similar fate. One night when we were youngsters, we went out with our instruments to a neighbouring favela to give a concert. Driving a car was quite normal for us, despite our youth. When we arrived at a police check they claimed that I had stolen all these instruments. One of the policemen held a gun to my head and said: "Boy, can you prove that these are really your instruments?" I was shaking all over and was sure that he would shoot us all if I did not play. I took my cavaquinho, a small guitar — the first instrument I learnt to play, and with the gun to my head, I played for my life. When the policeman heard the music, he slowly removed the gun. Since that moment I have known how deeply music can touch someone. In the meantime, I play 40 instruments, and our band won prizes and today performs throughout the country.

Tool of Change

For me, music became a tool of change, of transformation. We set up a music cellar in our parents' house, where we also gave lessons. My father has always supported us. Hundreds of children and young people have gone through our School of Music since 1990. Many of them have left the drug scene and, through music, found purpose to their lives. More and more people were making music, but we had no way to make recordings. In 2004, we opened our first improvised studio. We now have eight professionally equipped rooms and receive more than 300 musicians every month. In 2010, we organised a Favela Music Festival with 30 bands, it was a huge success. It should help to change the perception of the favela as a violent and terrible place, so that you can see its beautiful aspects. We can live together in peace!

We have sought other ways in which young people can find an expression for their dreams so that they may find their path in life, and also offer work with videos and movies.

Photo: Simon du Vinage

Building a Permaculture Garden in a favela house:
a step towards freedom.

115

Through art, we experience freedom, but nevertheless our reality is harsh. There is little work. At times we have electricity but no water, then vice versa. The food is unhealthy. We almost never see something green growing. My kids played in the narrow apartment, because the streets were run by drug dealers and gangs. And as the houses are not official, they can always be demolished by the government. We knew we had to do something, but didn't know what. My wife Hellem, my brother Fabio and other friends and band members pooled their money and funded my trip to Europe. Amongst other places, I visited Tamera in Portugal and saw things that I had never heard of before: permaculture, solar energy, ecovillages and much more.

Favela da Paz

During this time I had a dream. I saw all the people in our street — and there are 3,000 people — all generations happily living with permaculture, solar energy and a lot of music. When I came back, I wrote a new Samba Song: 'Favela da Paz'. In it, I describe a green area, not rich, but independent and free. The song was a hit and helped us find a way to realise the dream. Supporters were found. Lush Company from England, the Global Campus from Portugal, and the Elos Center of São Paulo brought money, international know-how and helpers.

Our family home — an 'unofficial' favela house which has had a new storey built on it with each succeeding generation — has now been turned into an ecological model house! Friends from Europe came and built a solar shower. The luxury of having a hot shower for as long as we want quickly made news in the neighbourhood. We established a permaculture garden on our roof, which gets soaked by rain water and therefore keeps itself watered. In our street, where green was rarely seen, the neighbours now collect the seeds from fruits to see them germinate in our roof garden.

And a year later, friends came from the Global Campus and built a mini biogas plant. It works like an artificial cow's stomach: the food scraps and content of the compost toilet are digested and produce methane gas for cooking. Our neighbours are amazed when they see the gas flame burn for the first time: "A miracle", they exclaim.

We regularly invite neighbours to our open house to show them what's new. And we invent other days, such as 'Children's Day', where we invite the street kids. They can come and play, paint themselves, draw pictures and simply be.

Community Wishes

For many years we have invited the neighbours and schools in the district to a concert on a monthly basis. In the neighbourhood concert of October 2013, Paulo Mellett, Ruth Andrade and the Elos Center played with us the "Oasis Game". We launched a survey among residents of the neighbourhood and asked: What do you wish for the most? Most answered: that the children can play outside again. But also: that trees should grow in the quarter. And that finally — after years — the garbage should be collected. That was the initiation of an action that changed the whole neighbourhood. Many people from the favela joined in.

Photo: Simon du Vinage

Connecting the neighbours and introducing them to new ideas of sustainability, organic food and energy.

117

In February 2014, we celebrated the opening of a jointly established playground with a folk festival, samba, and a local market. The trees that we planted are still small. But the garden in the courtyard has had its first harvest already. And then came what many have been waiting for over half their lives: the city actually sent a garbage disposal truck!!

I dream that in the future all favelas will turn into peace favelas and I would like to thank everyone who has supported us.

Keywords for Solution Library :

Urban permaculture — bringing nature back into the cities
Oasis Game — co-creating miracles from community dreams
Day of the Children — putting children at the centre of the community
solution.ecovillage.org

The Cultivation of Culture

Tenondé Porã / Brazil

The community of the indigenous tribe Tenondé Porã is located within
São Paulo city, and is connected to the Latin-American ecovillage network.
After living with the community, Henny Freitas realises that even though
it is besieged in the largest metropolis of the Southern Hemisphere, the
beautiful and sustainable elements of genuine and timeless indigenous
culture are truly alive here. Henny is a journalist who has been investigating
and documenting sustainable approaches within intentional communities
around South America and Oceania since 2008. During the 'Llamado de la
Montaña', a sustainability conference which took place in Colombia in 2012,
she participated in the process of forming CASA (Council of Sustainable
Settlements of the Americas) and has been involved in writing articles for
the GEN newsletter ever since.

Photo: Henry Freitas

One of the elders in the indigenous village that hosted our writers.

Henny Freitas

Following the philosophy of the Native American Iroquois Confederacy, in which chiefs must consider the impacts of every action taken for seven generations ahead, the Brazilian indigenous tribes have been fighting from one generation to another to keep their language and customs alive whilst living amongst the colonising 'white' civilisation.

Long before the arrival of the Portuguese in 1500, the first inhabitants of Brazil lived in aldeias (villages), deep within the ancient forests, spread across the four edges of the country. It is suggested that in the 16th century, the whole territory was occupied by up to 4 million inhabitants belonging to over 1,000 separate indigenous tribes.

According to anthropologist and writer, Darcy Ribeiro (1957), during the first half of the 20th century, the indigenous population was estimated to be around 200,000 people. A quick sum shows that in only 4 centuries the native Brazilians suffered a decline of 95%. Today, this figure is changing. Studies show that since the start of the 21stcentury most indigenous tribes have been growing at a rate of about 3.5% per year.

Anthropologists, demographers and health care professionals wonder whether the rise in population is a result of indigenous people living within demarked territories, having better access to medical assistance and increasing fertility, or whether it is in fact the result of a conscious decision to pursue a demographic recovery.

Philosophy in Practice

Despite speculation, there is still time for the Brazilian indigenous communities to put their Native Northern American comrades' philosophy into practice. That is, if the 'white' civilisation stop interfering.

Tenondé Porã is one of the three Guarani tribes located in São Paulo city. The tribe is also besieged in one of the largest and most green areas of its 96 districts because the area is being threatened by the construction of what would be the third airport in the capital. In order for us to enter and document their rich culture, multiple telephone and email conversations are exchanged. After an initial visit and long talk with a tribal ambassador, a period of stay is finally organised for us.

Backpacks packed, equipment tested and a lift arranged, we arrive! But it is not to be as simple as it seemed. Our honesty, integrity and intention all need to be proven during two long hours of eye-to-eye meeting with the Cacique (Chief) Timóteo Verá Popyguá and two other leaders of the tribe.

When the talk is over, the day has already given way to night and, even though we still don't know if we can stay, accommodation is provided for us in an empty village house for that first night. It is not until the next morning that we are given final approval to explore the local culture more.

: Henry Freitas

*The Tenondé community tries to protect the natural paradise
inside the municipality of São Paulo.*

Cock-a-doodle-doo

We wake up at the crack of dawn with the chortling of the roosters. After composing and printing out a contract document stating our intention, we are ready to present ourselves to the cacique again. The paperwork is read and signed by us all and our passport into the daily life of the community is metaphorically stamped and granted.

Tenondé Porã is the largest indigenous tribe of Guarani ethnicity in São Paulo city. The community was formed around 1930 by a group of 6 families. After 1960, more family members started to arrive from various regions inside and outside Brazil. The current cacique is an example of this migration. Mr Verá Popyguá arrived from Paraná (Southern Brazil) in 1983 to live in an area that would be demarcated and officially sanctioned just a few years later, in 1987. Today the aldeia has about 120 families sharing a space of 26 ha with a population of 700.

On a rainy afternoon, near the end of our stay, the cacique, Timóteo, sits down with us to explain more about the Guarani culture, diffused between Brazil, Paraguay, Argentina, Bolivia and Uruguay. "Traditionally, the Guaranis didn't have chiefs to govern their tribes. Our leaders have always been the *Pajés* (shamans). They are our spiritual guides and counsellors".

He explains to us that the term cacique was coined in order to name the person in charge of representing the tribe outside its borders, to the *Jeruas*, literally meaning 'mouth with hair' — making reference to the moustache and beard of the European conquerors. Today Jerua is a generic reference to any non-indigenous person.

As the cacique of Tenondé Porã, Timóteo's biggest role within the community is to make sure that the rights of its citizens are respected. He also says that being a representative is an opportunity to act as a voice for their culture and traditions to be correctly understood. "Culture is what we cultivate. The Guaranis have a millenary knowledge. Our wisdom, as well as our traditions and language, have been passed on by our relatives from generation to generation".

Jaguars, toucans, coatis...

During our stay at the aldeia, the house we are offered on the first night becomes our home for the following week. With a wood fireplace and simple furnishings, we find ourselves comfortable and self-sufficient, cooking our own meals and happily entertaining visitors with our warm hearth and fresh coffee.

We live next to a beautiful family who keep many of the traditions alive. Our neighbours are a loving couple and their two children — a smiley girl of 5 and an enchanting boy of 2. The father, Isac, is a timber craftsman and shows us that the art of carving wild animals is in his blood. The proof is clear as we closely follow his skilled work as he transforms pieces of tree-trunk into incredible jaguars, toucans, owls and coatis, to name but a few.

Our door is always open, and our new friend, his children and many others join us by our fire. Often the kids come from school, telling us of their day and questioning us about our Western ways.

At Tenondé Porã, children between 1 and 6 years old are taught by villagers — speaking only the Guarani Mbya language, learning about their traditions, culture and the world around them. After their 7th birthday, combined with their cultural teachings, they also learn Brazilian Portuguese and have external teachers coming to educate them in a more conventional schooling method. In this way children receive a blended education giving priority to their own teachings and philosophy.

Together with a traditional midwife facility and a modern medical clinic, the educational centre is located at the heart of the aldeia. Mothers are welcome to participate in the school's activities, including: singing, dancing, story-telling, along with spending time visiting the local Mata Atlântica to study the forest's diversity and significance, amongst many other subjects. Whilst visiting the school, we arrange to return in the evening in order to share our views about sustainability with the older teenagers.

We are introduced to the other features of the tribal grounds and led across the land by Lísio Lima — one of the leaders of the community. Lísio was the ambassador we spoke to on our initial visit and was also present with us at the two-hour conversation with the cacique upon our arrival.

He himself is a talented craftsman, making many types of jewellery and artefacts, which he uses to promote cultural awareness whilst presenting talks and lectures at conferences and fairs all over the country.

During this walk and talk we get a real feel for the land and find many positive footprints upon it. The highlight of the expedition is our arrival at a self-built bridge, constructed with light logs perched on forked branches, connected without nails or bindings. They use the passage to cross the depths of a reed-filled dam called 'Billings', where they fish from an elevated platform amongst the frog calls.

Photo: Henry Freitas

Music and prayer are inherent parts of the traditional culture that the community is trying to maintain.

House of Prayer

Once we get back to the community centre, it is already time to cook our dinner before preparing ourselves for the evening. Every night of our stay at the aldeia we take part in an extensive ceremony. This is perhaps the most culturally alive aspect of village life for this large spiritual family who have warmly 'adopted' us.

On our first night at the *Casa de Reza* (house of prayer), where the nightly ritual takes place, the pajé Papa sheds tears when mentioning the dream he had about people coming to stay with them for a certain period of time to understand more about their culture and traditions. We humbly accept our role as temporary residents and speak at length to the congregation about our joy at being there.

There are things that happen in a place that words cannot describe and only those who are present can truly understand. These nights, spent clouded by thick tobacco smoke and surrounded by devotion and ceremony, are something we will never forget. They have embedded in our mind and hearts an understanding of Guarani culture that is as alive as the blood flowing through its people's veins.

Keywords for Solution Library:
Community Midwifery — enabling women to give birth at their homes
Traditional Rituals — reconnecting with the spirit of nature
Traditional schooling methodology/practices — passing on indigenous wisdom
solution.ecovillage.org

The Decision for Life

Peace Community San José de Apartadó / Colombia

In March 1997 brutal fighting took hold in the region of Apartadó in the north of Colombia. Guerrillas and paramilitary forces chased the farmers off their land. Both groups use a terrible technique known as 'burnt earth' that destroys houses, forests and rivers. In the small village of San José de Apartadó around 1000 farmers, trade unionists and refugees have come together to form a peace community. They adhere to rules of nonviolence, determined to stay neutral between the two fronts, and work with tools of peaceful resistance. The immediate danger is all too real: over the years violence has claimed the lives of 200 members of the peace community. Every family in the village has at least one murdered member whether a parent, child or sibling. The state does not protect them; on the contrary, they are suspected of being supporters of the guerrillas and have therefore been classified as outlaws.

Photo: David Osthoff

Eduar Lanchero

In spite of every adversity the peace community continues. Together they succeed in growing organic cocoa and bananas. International support helps to protect the community. A school was initially established, followed by a health clinic and a medicinal herb garden, a small chocolate factory and a solar power plant. The village is free from weapons and has become legendary amongst the surrounding guerrillas, military, paramilitary and drug lords. Eduar Lanchero accompanied the peace community from its establishment until his death in June 2012.

Eduar Lanchero

A long history of violence precedes the establishment of the peace community. The Uraba region always balanced precariously between hopes of peace on one side and global capitalist interests on the other. The government of Colombia has mainly sided with foreign capital. As long ago as 1929, the United Fruit Company — later re-named as Chiquita — was established in the region. They needed land and workers and therefore started to displace land-owning farmers. As landless people they were then forced to work for low wages in inhumane working conditions on the plantations. When they organised in unions, the companies started to fight them. Military documents today provide evidence that paramilitary units were already established by the early 1960s. They murdered trade union leaders, ousted farmers and threatened workers. Since then war has reigned. The guerrillas became active in the region only from 1978 onwards.

Community Establishment

By 1996 the remnants of organised civil society had been annihilated. People were helpless and their only hope of survival was to leave. This horror made possible the current situation we live in today. By attacking San José — the last stronghold of the left wing party Union Patriotica — the paramilitary groups wanted to demonstrate that they had conquered the entire region. It was around this time that the peace community was established.

On the 23rd of March, 1997, representatives from 32 hamlets of the municipality of San José gathered and declared themselves to be the neutral peace community of San José de Apartadó. The Red Cross, the Commission for Peace and Justice, as well as other international witnesses were present. I, myself came with the Inter-Church Commission for Justice and Peace to San José. Their decision was the only logical choice in the face of this violence. However we sensed how risky the intentions of the campesinos would be. I could not talk them into taking this step while not taking the same risk as they did. And so I became one of them.

Core Principles

The logic of the guerrillas, paramilitary and military is simple: if you are not on their side you are on the enemy's side. The peace community was the first national example of a neutral entity to declare that it did not want to work with either party. Four days after the declaration of the community, on the 27th of March, 1997, a series of massacres, attacks and bombings started across the whole area. The villages emptied out. Those who survived, a population of 6,000 people, fled, and 320 ended up living in San José. We changed our focus: we were no longer defending our land, but also our lives.

Photo: Ludwig Schramm

All members of the Peace Community help to build the village.

The peace community was an obstacle to the government claiming our land. But the peace community also became a problem for the guerrillas because we were the first ones who clearly said: "We do not follow your orders. We do not support you and want nothing to do with you". And so we became the target of all sides. The logic of this war is to contaminate the population with fear. But this community stood upright even after their leaders were murdered. Instead of panicking, the peace community created their core principles:

- No support or co-operation with any armed conflict parties
- Peaceful and nonviolent resistance
- No weapons
- No drugs (no cultivation, no dealing or use)

- No alcohol
- Mutual support (e.g. during food cultivation, health)
- Transparency within the group.

Birthing a New Lifestyle

We recognised a fundamental theme: although we stand up against the armed groups, these are not the only ones that murder. It is the logic behind the system, the entire way of life which is violent. Therefore we decided that we would have to live, think and work differently, if we wanted to bring forth life. One aspect that had to change was land ownership. Land has to be maintained and cared for by the community. We also realised that fear makes people controllable and exploitable. The farmers were in fear when they worked alone. So we started to work in groups.

The armed groups and the government were constantly lying, so we realised that we had to be transparent. We needed to learn to speak the truth amongst ourselves with no regard to the consequences.

The central element that lies at the root of our principles is the search for justice. But there was no justice within the current system's logic, so we started global partnerships with other resistance groups. Together we can build a peaceful society, a non-violent world. This means more than simply stopping war, but also meeting criteria that inspire and ensure life.

In February 2005, Luis Eduardo Guerra, speaker of the peace community, as well as eight other people, were brutally killed by the paramilitary. In the camouflage of apparent protection, the government announced that they would establish a military station in San José. For us this was not a sign of protection but rather the opposite: we assumed for many years that the military and paramilitary worked very closely together. Just a short while ago this assumption was proven in court. To live in the same village as the military was not an option for us: that would have been the end of neutrality. We decided to collectively leave the village, as an act of unity. A few kilometres further down the road we secured some land and established a new village on the green meadows along a river. We call it San Josécito — the small San José. We built homes, meeting spaces, a health clinic, a small cocoa factory, a school, a library, a house for international supporters, and also solar power plants, to be independent from the government's electricity supply.

Importance of Hope

Due to the fact that we are living a new life, death gains a different meaning too. Death bows down to life. This thought helps us overcome the horrific trauma that armed groups created. The state and the armed units say: "We did everything possible, yet we could not destroy them". They ask themselves what they can still do to us. In their blindness, the murderers cannot see that they can do anything they want to us, but the community will still be there, as long as pain can be transformed into hope.

Photo: Ludwig Schramm

In the middle of a civil war, between the front lines of guerrilla and paramilitary, there is an oasis of non-violence and peace.

129

And what is hope? It appears when we stop hating our murderers. In our daily lives we boldly say to them that their murdering does not bring them victory over us. At the beginning we wanted to change the world; today we see that we have changed the world because we stayed unified as one community.

I believe that we can make it. We need training and education for youth so that they may not be tempted by the plastic fruits of the city that at the end of the day squeeze no juice. We need a type of internal educational system, a kind of political monastery where we as the community come together to learn alternative methods outside the daily fight for survival. High up in the mountains, in the small hamlet of Mulatos, the place where Luis Eduardo was murdered, we have started building such a place.

We must help one another. That is the most important message. It does not matter how many we are: what matters is that we are building the new world with every day that we live. We cannot build this other world tomorrow, we have to build it today.

We made a decision. Our decision is life. And it is life itself that corrects and leads us.

Noella Tuberquia, 35, works in the fields, knows medicinal plants and studies most Saturdays in the community school. A few years ago her village 'la Cristalina' got caught up in the crossfire between the army and the guerrillas. Her youngest daughter and mother in law were shot. "The farmers in Colombia have always been in danger of being attacked and displaced. They steal our land, our money and food supply and many of us were killed. Yet the peace community is still there; the kids learn from a young age what it means to live on the land and not to allow oneself to be chased off. The farmers move in small groups across their fields to protect one another. One day a week we have a community day where everybody comes together to work. The solidarity within the peace community is our biggest survival skill."

José Lopez, 24, is a teacher in the school that has branches in the different hamlets that comprise the peace community. He walks hours every day through the forests in order to teach at the different schools. As a youth he was nearly sucked into becoming a guerrilla. "On the radio we receive daily invites from various armed groups to join them. When I was 15 my first girlfriend broke up with me. This was such a big pain for me that I wanted to leave everything behind. I wanted to go off into the mountains where I had some friends among the guerrillas. Some joined because they liked it, others out of revenge because their parents were killed by the paramilitary. In my case it was simply a broken heart. Yet God and my community made it clear to me that this was not a path for a young man in search of peace. With the guerrillas I would have never found peace, only war. Now I am happy to be part of the peace community and work in its educational sector."

Keywords for Solution Library:
University of Resistance — sharing knowledge and skills for non-violent resistance
Medicinal Gardens — strengthening local sovereignty in healthcare
solution.ecovillage.org

Building Community and Resisting Globalisation

Comuna Tola Chica / Ecuador

Comuna Tola Chica is a traditional community in the Tumbaco Valley of northern Ecuador and a member of the ecovillage network of Latin America. Ramiro Azaña, now 40, has lived in Tola Chica since he was a child.*

Ramiro Azaña

Ramiro Azaña

In truth, the origins of our community can be traced back to our ancestors. The word Comuna translates roughly as Commune, but it has an older, ancestral meaning, and the Comunas date back to pre-colonial indigenous society, when private property did not exist and our communities shared land and decision-making in regional community groups.

Under colonial Spanish rule, most of our land was appropriated and redistributed to new Spanish landowners. However, some groups have maintained some autonomy and land stewardship and have survived until today. Our community has a level of autonomy in organisation and land usage that is recognised under Ecuadorian law, dating back to a 1937 law, which legally recognised the right for indigenous communities to maintain their autonomous communal structures. Comuna Tola Chica was first formally recognised as a legal entity in 1944, but the official founding of the Comuna dates back to the 1920s.

Life in the Comuna

The Comuna is home to over 60 families with a total of about 400 people. Land ownership is communal and decisions are taken by a democratic system, with an organisational council elected by the community to guide procedures.

The community land is divided into three zones:
1) Offices and Education 2) Residential and small gardens 3) Large-scale organic agriculture and reforestation. This third zone is the largest, and no construction is permitted there.

We all share the following responsibilities: political decisions, water issues, large-scale food production areas, a sports area, the community school, event centre, training and a future tourism project. Other communal activities include two annual festivals that bring the entire community together, and 12 mingas (collective work days) each year.

From the beginning, the minga has been crucial to maintain our community. At least one member of the family must participate or the family must pay a fine. Our mingas are a source of unity, learning and seeking together to make progress for the community. Our biggest miracle is that of working and living together through all the experiences of life, together with our friends, partners, children and families to ensure the continuity of the comuna. This is the adventure of life, as the comuna grows and we demonstrate that this form of life is still possible today.

Resisting Globalisation

The history of the Comunas in Ecuador is a story of resisting both colonisation and integration into the modernising and urbanising Ecuadorian society.

In our daily life, our community is trying to stop what globalisation is bringing into our region. We constantly struggle to maintain our way of life, while Quito, the big city, keeps growing. Currently in our valley there are two mega development projects, a new highway and a new international airport, which will bring lots of new settlers and noise to the area, and new laws, so we are once again preparing to defend ourselves, in the sense that we wish our community to survive.

Photo: Ryan Luckey

The community comes together to work, to fight against globalisation and to celebrate.

Since our beginning, we have looked to preserve and protect the local environment from development, and to protect our rights and our ability to live a more natural life on the land, as we have traditionally lived. We are proud of who we are and how we live, preserving our natural surroundings. Our way of life allows us to live without working against nature or anyone else. We are farmers, and since the beginning have always wanted to protect our environment, our seeds and our way of life.

More recently, since the year 2000, we have put more emphasis on bringing together the ancestral knowledge of our elders with modern knowledge and innovative solutions.

Reforestation with Native Plants

One of the biggest projects we have taken on is reforesting the land, much of which has been burned in intentional fires started by neighbours, who plant eucalyptus as a cash crop. In the past, we have had to put out these fires, so now we are always on alert as guardians. We have to defend the land from people who don't understand conservation and don't understand why we want to plant and protect the native flora.

We have made it clear that we aren't against the exotic species per se, especially eucalyptus, which is very common here. However we are against planting exotic species in large-scale production. In order to address this conflict, we have organised workshops and events to raise awareness about our reforestation projects. Through these actions, our experiences are shared. Then we let time pass and ultimately people realise that we are right, that native species should be preserved in their places of origin.

We are using our knowledge to recover deforested areas and to plant native plants in biological corridors. As a community we have fully reforested 5 acres of land, with 7 more in recovery, and we hope to be able to reforest 50 acres in the future. The reforestation work is hugely important, because this region suffers a severe dry season and needs trees to hold water in the ecosystem to support the human, plant and animal communities.

Photo: Ryan Luc

Children and young people learn from an early age about sustainable technologies and organic gardening

Sharing Experience to Inspire Others

I am an accountant, but now I have trained to manage native plant nurseries and reforestation projects. This has not been a change for me, because I always lived on the land and I always had knowledge in my hands. But I decided to share this knowledge, and of course, along the way I have learned much more. My only change has been to work with more determination to defend nature from the damage that we human beings have caused. We are very intelligent beings, but in the end we are not using our intelligence very well!

In times of crisis, our call is to raise awareness about how to live more harmoniously with nature. We offer everyone the chance to come and experience our way of life, so people can learn and put this into practice. We receive hundreds of visitors every year, both locals and international visitors. But these changes have to be motivated from within, they can't be an obligation.

Being held in a network is important for everything else we do. The truth is that if things continue the way they are going today, hope is far away. But thanks to these networks, we see that more and more people share our vision of living a life that treads softly on our earth. So let's keep getting stronger: with more and more of us, we can bring back hope for a better world than the one we have now.

135

Our Community Elder

We live in the foothills of the Ilalo volcano, a landscape that rises up to meet the sky in curves and crevices. Our land ranges from 2,450m (8,000 feet) above sea level to 3,200m (10,500 feet) above sea level up at the top.

I like to take our visitors up to the top of the mountain, to visit our community elder. We take a short drive up a rugged dirt road, and stop to look out over the Tumbaco Valley. The air is very dry up here, and vegetation is low, mostly grasses. We walk through ecologically damaged areas, and then we walk through the reforested area, where native plants are reclaiming territory. The green mass of trees, vines and bushes form a stark contrast to the dry grasslands and fields in the surrounding area.

Then we go to visit our community elder, our sacred tree. It's a huila tree, belonging to the Arrayan family. Using carbon dating, we have determined this tree to be 1,814 years old!

The huila tree rises just a few metres off the ground, and at first glance doesn't call too much attention to itself. But if you close your eyes and tune in to the more subtle energies, you can feel it: this is a wise and ancient tree. It's seen generations come and go. It has stood watch as the valley below has developed, at first little by little and now at an alarming speed.

What does the huila tree think of the new highway passing close by on the way to the new Quito international airport? What does it think of the people who burn the hillsides to clear native plants in order to expand commercial eucalyptus production?

The huila tree doesn't speak Spanish, or even Quechua. That's why we have to speak for it. We have to tell people that there is an alternative to the current development model. We can learn to live in harmony with nature and with each other, and keep alive our cultural traditions. We stand for a different vision of society, one in which sustainable communities are the norm, not the 'alternative.'

Keywords for Solution Library:
Minga — sharing community tasks
Collective Land Ownership — re-establishing the commons
solution.ecovillage.org

*The text is based on an interview with Ryan Luckey.

163 Years after Slavery: Recognising AfroColombian Communities' Rights

Islas del Rosario / Colombia

After many years of legal struggle, an Afro-Colombian community has been recognised as having the right to be owners of the Islands of Rosario in the Colombian Caribbean. Their vision is to transition to an ecovillage, and revitalise the knowledge and skills of their traditions.

Ever de la Rosa Morales

Ever de la Rosa Morales

My name is Ever de la Rosa Morales, leader of the Afro-Colombian community of Islas del Rosario. We are around 1,000 people living on 27 small islands in the Colombian Caribbean. After a legal struggle lasting eight years, and a long history of exclusion and discrimination, on May 8th 2014 something historic happened: the government of Colombia finally acknowledged that an Afro-Colombian community has rights to the islands it has inhabited for generations.

The history of our community started a long time ago with the painful process of slavery. People from all around Africa were shipped to Cartagena to be sold as slaves. Around the year 1600 more than 80 different languages were spoken in the main port. Some of the slaves managed to escape and found a way to survive in remote areas of the country.

Others were forced to work on haciendas until the abolition of slavery in 1851. Once liberated, they occupied lands and started to grow food, to fish and to revitalise their cultures as best they could. The Rosario Islands have been inhabited by Afro-descendant people for more than 300 years, ever since fishermen from the continental town of Barú began to grow crops there while they were resting during fishing expeditions. They built very simple huts and stayed for a while, then travelled again to the mainland.

Conflicting Interests

This had been the way for many years, but then wealthier people from the continent started to fish in the area and asked the fishermen to take them to the best spots to find special fish. Suddenly, the land that previously lacked an owner, but belonged to everyone, started to have a price. The beauty of the islands, the coral reefs, and wonderful scenery were all attractive. Since then economic interest in the islands grew rapidly and our ancestors started to trade and sold big portions of land.

The area surrounding the islands was declared a National Natural Park in 1977. At that time I was a young boy living between Isleta and Isla Grande, the two main inhabited islands, and Cartagena, which is the nearest city. I was learning to fish and loved sports; soon I started to organise teams and games with other children and later with young people. I think my passion to work with and for the people began in those early days when I started to feel the trust that the community had in me.

The first challenges I faced as an elected leader were related to the lack of interest of the government in Afro-communities. For them, we were invisible and our needs were never taken into account in governmental plans. I started to meet with people and institutions that could help us to win access, initially, to education and health. I began to understand that we were in a very vulnerable situation. As a community, we didn't have legal recognition of permanent residence and the government was looking for ways to evict us.

In 1984, a legal process started. The government argued that we had illegally appropriated the islands. This ongoing process intensified around 2005. One of the main arguments was the importance and beauty of the ecosystems. The government saw us as a threat to nature, not taking into consideration that we had cared for the ecological richness of this area for centuries and that we, as natives, can be considered a part of these beautiful ecosystems. In contrast, the authorities seemed to be unable to address the

138

real environmental threats coming from mass tourism, industrial fisheries and pollution of the waters.

Photo: Margarita Zetelius

The Afro-Colombian community on the Rosario Islands wants to maintain its cultural heritage in everyday life.

139

The Legal/Rights Opportunity

Slowly, we discovered that in the Colombian Constitution of 1991, Colombia was recognised as a multiethnic and multicultural country. In 1993, the Afro-Colombian communities acquired legal tools to demand recognition of our rights. During different activities that I attended, I met people with great knowledge and experience in this field. In a collective effort we invited them to the community for talks and workshops. One of the decisions we took was to create a central town to become more visible to the external institutions. In 2000, we took back land that had been abandoned by a rich owner. There we created our central town Orika. The whole community participated in what is called 'minga' (community solidarity in action) by our indigenous communities; some were cooking, others were building...

Our political organisation, which used to be a Communal Action Board (Junta de Acción Comunal), was transformed into the Community Council of Islas del Rosario (Consejo Comunitario de las Islas del Rosario), which I'm currently representing. We had a beautiful process of reconstructing the history of the community with the support of numerous organisations and people who believed in our struggle. With these maps, in 2006 we officially requested the Collective Title (Land Tenure) of the two islands, Isla Grande and Isleta. Several legal complications arose and our application was denied twice. Many people advised us to accept what the government was offering; individual contracts for the use of the land for a given time period. Some government representatives threatened that the community would be evicted by force if we did not accept this offer.

After facing several threats, I received a call to inform us that the army was coming to evacuate members of the community. We organised ourselves and phoned our lawyers. When the army arrived we were there, defending ourselves and our land until the letter from the lawyer arrived. Over the years, I also received several threat calls. It took courage to keep going. Eventually, after a long process, the Constitutional Court decided in our favour.

The process has been full of miracles. We attended the right events, got to know exactly the people who could help us and were willing to do so. We gained the trust of the community and their commitment to see the process through. We found the strength and dignity to confront those with great economic and decision making power. Now we have become an inspiration to other communities, which is very fulfilling. We hope that miracles, trust and strength continue to manifest so that every community can also accomplish what is its right: having ownership of their land and the autonomy to develop in their own unique way.

Tradition and innovation towards sustainability and sovereignty

Over the past 13 years, we have been involved in several biodiversity conservation and development projects. Some of the main initiatives include: alternative economic activities, ecovillage design, waste management and ecotourism enterprises, solar panel installation, composting toilets, permaculture home gardens, environmental education, communitarian water storage and greening of schools. Each of these projects allowed us to build on the wealth of our traditions. Nevertheless, we feel that the connection to our African origins needs to be revitalised. Currently we are working on a development plan from our perspective to manifest our dreams.

Community Ecotourism forms a core element of our current activities. We are generating educational activities for both visitors and our own people. In the main plaza of Orika, we built our 'House of Culture', which has become the heart of these activities. Since 2014 we have been hosting different programmes, such as the EDE course (Ecovillage Design Education). People from other communities who see what we do are inspired, and we share our experiences with them, so that a network of friendships is growing.

Photo: Margarita Zetelius

Rosario Island is one of the few paradises left in the Caribbean: instead of mass tourism, the wellbeing of the community and its children are the main aim of the development.

141

The community of the Islas del Rosario recognises the importance of integrating traditional and innovative practices. We see ourselves as an ecovillage in an eco-region in a constant process of increasing the quality of life of the community. We are taking care of the ecosystems that are taking care of our territory for us and the next generations.

For more than 18 years I have been working to promote the recognition of Afro-Colombian communities' rights, to lead the process of transition from being invisible to becoming a visible, prosperous, sustainable community. All my life, I have been active in promoting values of dignity and equality within a difficult environment of racism and discrimination. Now I see that all these efforts have been fruitful, we can inspire and help other communities to find solutions in a changing world.

Keywords for Solution Library:

Participatory Action Research — learning from communities
Community Ecotourism — inviting visitors in a way that helps to protect the environment
solution.ecovillage.org

Balance Between Old and Young

Sirius Community / Massachusetts, USA

Sirius community was founded in September 1978 by former members of the Findhorn Community in Scotland wishing to establish a similar community in their American homeland. Its foundation is spiritual, but in a non-sectarian manner that allows for each person to find their own way. The shared expression reflects reverence for all Life and a willingness to live in accord with this intention as much as possible. The community thus employs ecologically sustainable methods of living and a consensus-style governance process, striving to honor all that is.

Daniel Greenberg and his family.

Daniel Greenberg

My personal journey into community began with a robbery. On the evening of September 9, 1989, we packed our camper van so we could leave the next morning for a tour of intentional communities across North America. My partner (and now wife), Monique, was producing a video documentary on contemporary communes and I was writing a doctoral thesis on children and education in these settings.

At dawn, we were excited to hit the road after months of planning but were devastated when we found someone had broken into our van and stolen everything — our clothes, Monique's video camera, my computer, guitar, even my bootleg Grateful Dead tapes. All gone.

After a week of recovering from the shock, dealing with insurance companies, and debating whether we should even go at all, we took a deep breath and started off again. Our lives have never been the same since. I learned more on the first day I set foot in an actual community than in the two years I had spent studying them, and we visited over 30 in nine months.

Monique was inspired to become a midwife while visiting the Farm and later completed her documentary called 'Follow the Dirt Road'. We discovered the many uses of soybeans. I learned how to wear a skirt and weave a hammock. We had long conversations about everything from attachment parenting to polyamory. And we came to really love living in community.

Children and Youth

I discovered children in communities grow up both savvy and sassy. They see adults building houses, relationships and political structures. They also see arguments, tears and social faux pas. Adults become demystified and more human, and their relationships extend beyond their nuclear families as they grow into global citizens.

We then moved to Findhorn in Scotland, and spent a wonderful year working with children and families. Half way through, a friend brought over some college students and I witnessed each of them 'Pop!' — their lives transformed by Findhorn's visions and practices — much like what had happened to me during our travels. Something clicked. I woke up one night with goose bumps and a vision to bring more young adults to these ideal campuses, to learn about living well and lightly in harmony with each other and the planet.

We returned to the US and in 1999, I started Living Routes, which partnered with University of Massachusetts Amherst, to run 'study abroad' programs in ecovillages around the world. In the end, over 1,500 Living Routes students woke up to new possibilities for themselves and the planet at Findhorn (Scotland), Auroville (India), Kibbutz Lotan (Israel), Huehuecoyotl (Mexico), EcoYoff (Senegal), Crystal Waters (Australia) and more.

It was life-changing work. After spending time living and learning in one of these ecovillages, students could never again say, "It can't be done", because they experienced *doing it*. Each student had to ask him- or herself, "What am I going to do? How can I make a difference in my own life and in my own community?"

We also asked ourselves these questions and in 1998, after visiting and living in so many communities, we decided to settle down at Sirius, a spiritual community, education center and ecovillage in western Massachusetts.

Founding Sirius

Sirius was founded in 1978 by two brothers, Bruce and Gordon Davidson, and their partners, Linda Reimer and Corinne McLaughlin. After being members of Findhorn for about five years, they were invited to tour the US and offer workshops with Peter Caddy, one of Findhorn's founders.

After arriving in America, both Bruce and Gordon had an intuition to start a community in the US. They were staying with a woman who mentioned that the land across the street was for sale. But it was mid-December and they decided to search for land in a warmer climate.

They traveled all around the country offering workshops and looking for land, but never found anything. Bruce then returned to Findhorn because Linda was there and pregnant with their first daughter and because he was head of the Core Group that was then dealing with the difficult transition of leadership beyond Peter.

Gordon and Corrine later came back to where they started and, while meditating, Gordon received guidance to buy the land across the street. The owner requested a $30,000 deposit within three days, but the local bank wouldn't consider a loan because, not only had they no money, they didn't even have addresses in the U.S.

The next day, they went to a communities' gathering and, amazingly, one person gave them a $10,000 donation and another offered a $20,000 loan on the spot. The landowner liked their vision and the fact that they weren't going to chop the land into parcels, so he gave them a personal mortgage at half the current interest rate and half the market value. Gordon bought the ninety acres with a house and two garages for $70,000 and Bruce and Linda joined them six months later.

The community was named Sirius, after the brightest star in the sky, considered by some to be the source of love and wisdom for our planet. Sirius aims to honor the highest principles common to all sacred traditions — from Native American to New Age, from western mystery schools to eastern traditions, and everything in between. This spirituality is manifested through attunements before meetings and events, communion with nature in their gardens, full-moon meditations, yoga and Chi Kung in the Community Center, rituals at the Stone Circle and more.

Today, there are about 30 residents (a mix of members, exploring members, guests and renters) and another 150 would identify as members of the wider community known as Hearthstone Village (named in honor of seven Native American longhouse hearths in the area). And several thousand people visit Sirius each year for their bi-weekly Open Houses, monthly Work Exchange Weekends, seasonal holiday meals, cob oven pizza parties, and educational programs that range from permaculture to herbal medicine to spiritual book clubs. There are also 'Rota' lunches and dinners most days where people cook and share vegetarian, local, organic meals, often with food grown in Sirius's gardens and greenhouses.

Building green and energy-wise: gardening and harvesting solar energy in homes.

Like most communities, Sirius strives to balance a variety of needs and values. For example, while members choose their own diet, the community kitchen is strictly vegetarian. Decisions are made by consensus in Thursday Night Meetings, but there is also a Core Group that has authority around the community's membership, finances, and purpose and direction. Anyone can challenge a Core Group decision in which case it is discussed in the general meetings (often at length) and then brought back to the Core Group for reconsideration.

And, of course, things don't always work perfectly, especially in the early years when there were major conflicts between members, not least between Bruce and Gordon.

Like cleaning potatoes...

Monique and I moved across the road after a few years living at Sirius, when it became too challenging to juggle community, family and professional obligations. We began to notice and identify more with wider community members, many who had left for similar reasons. It's quite common for ecovillages to develop in this way as they become more mature and stable. But it can also be a challenge to expand their psychological 'bubbles' and maintain strong relationships with ex-members and others who choose to live near but not in the community.

In an effort to bridge this gap, we started weekly Hearthstone Kitchen meals at Sirius, which drew hundreds of locals and ex-members of Sirius back, some for the first time in years. Sirius also completed their public sauna in 2008, which is a wonderful place to melt old conflicts. It's a bit like the Japanese method of cleaning potatoes by putting them into a pot of water and stirring. By rubbing against each other in community, we tend to become a bit softer and less edgy over time.

Bruce suffered a major accident in 2010 while felling a tree and he and Linda have been slowly transitioning out of leadership in recent years. Fortunately, there is a solid group of members who are committed to growing themselves spiritually and expanding the community physically and socially. Several youth have been very active in the development of NextGEN, both in North America and internationally. And, in addition to the current windmills, photovoltaic arrays and ecological buildings (made of local timberframes, straw bales and cob), members are talking about creating a new guest lodge, a meditation space, new educational programs and possibly purchasing some adjoining property.

147

A main impetus of Sirius ecovillage is training for youth,
including NextGEN.

Sirius will continue to thrive, not only because of its competent and committed membership, but also because it is on the leading edge of where humanity is heading. It is easy to view ecovillages as eccentric, marginal and irrelevant to our dominant mainstream cultures, but if we step back, it becomes clear that it is our industrialised societies that are doomed to failure — as short, yet dramatic chapters in our planet's history. For 99.9% of our evolutionary history, humans lived in tribes. We are hardwired for community and for belonging to each other and our natural world. Sirius and other ecovillages are rekindling this deep need and knowing and they are helping us create new cultures and new stories in which we can truly experience our interbeing-ness, with each other and all life.

www.siriuscommunity.org

> Keyword for Solution Library:
> Earth Deeds — measuring carbon footprints and funding
> sustainability projects
> *solution.ecovillage.org*

The Edge Effect

EcoVillage Ithaca / USA

EcoVillage Ithaca, founded in 1991, is the largest ecovillage in the United States. Its 3 co-housing neighborhoods and 3 organic farms show university students and the mainstream public that the American way of life can be changed in small but significant ways, to enable people to live with more social and ecological sustainability. Liz Walker is one of the founders of EcoVillage Ithaca.

Liz Walker

Liz Walker

In 1990 I helped my colleague Joan Bokaer organize an environmental peace walk across the United States. My family and I joined 150 people from 6 different nations including Native Americans. During the Walk we travelled 3,000 miles across the US, starting in LA and ending up in NYC. On the way we planted trees, helped to start recycling programmes and met with school children, local businesses and churches. And in the middle of the walk my marriage fell apart. Painful as it was, my husband and I both decided to stay on with our two boys, then 4 and 7 years old. The walk taught all of us a tremendous amount about empowerment, persistence and patience, going through crises and the value of support, while walking 15 to

20 miles a day. We all felt: "Wow, if we can do this, we can do anything".

On the walk, Joan started dreaming about creating an ongoing community, and 6 months later she called and asked if I would like to help organize an ecovillage in Ithaca. It was an exciting idea, and after meditating I got a clear message that this is what I was meant to do. So, I left my home of 15 years in San Francisco and moved to Ithaca as a new single parent.

Ithaca is located in the beautiful Finger Lakes area of New York State, with lakes, rolling hills and lots of farms. Home to Cornell University, it is well known for its environmental concern. We had heard about other ecovillages starting around the world and chose the term 'ecovillage' so that we were seen to be part of this global network.

In June, 1991, we had a 5-day retreat to envision what we could create together. 100 people camped out under the stars by Cayuga Lake. At the beginning the retreat was a little rocky — Joan had done the most thinking about the project and it was clear that people did not want to follow a leader. They wanted to be working together as a team. There was tremendous energy. As the facilitator I felt like a surfer, riding the wave of excitement. We broke into small teams to start planning farms, buildings and educational programs. At the end of the five days, people didn't want to go home.

Buying Land, Design and Construction

We looked for land with good farming potential, and close to the city so that we could open to visitors. The piece of land we chose was 175 acres, 2 miles from downtown Ithaca.

We created a non-profit organization affiliated with Cornell University.

Joan and I were working long hours and had dozens of volunteers. Together we raised US$400,000, just by calling people and asking: "Would you like to invest in this vision?" I was amazed at the response. We used these loans to purchase the land on the Summer Solstice in 1992, exactly one year after the Envisioning Retreat. That night we camped out on the land.

We then spent a year in an intensive planning process with Cornell professors, graduate students, housewives, architects, ecologists... anybody who was interested got involved. Together we created a 10-page document, *The Guidelines for Development*, with sections on land and water use, neighborhoods, green buildings, transportation, farming and energy guidelines.

In 1996 we started building our first co-housing neighborhood. None of us had ever seen a co-housing community before. In November, my new partner, Jared, myself and the kids moved in along with 8 other families. Half of the homes were still under construction. We had an Open House with lots of visitors. That very evening a huge fire burned 8 of the homes to the ground as well as the Common House. Luckily no one was hurt, but it was a huge set-back.

The fire was shocking — and at the same time our community really pulled together and people helped each other out. With the insurance money we were able to pay for the cost of rebuilding. Nine months later we finished the neighborhood and everyone moved in.

Today we have 3 neighborhoods, and each has its own story. In 2015, with 100 homes our neighborhood development is complete.

In Co-housing neighorhoods, children always find friends to play with.

Community-Supported Agriculture

We have 3 organic farms on site, a very important part of our overall vision and mission. We use CSA (Community-Supported Agriculture) in which consumers pay the farmers at the beginning of the growing season, then get a weekly share of the harvest. Our first farm, West Haven Farm, has 11 acres and feeds 1,000 people during the season. Our second farm is 5 acres and is also run by a resident. It's a U-Pick berry farm, which has delicious strawberries, blackberries, blueberries and more. However it can be challenging as people need time to pick the berries.

Our third farm is part of our educational work. In the United States most farmers are 60 years old or more, which is very scary. I wonder what's going to happen to our food system in another 10 years. We are training young people to farm. Our incubator farm is 10 acres and is set aside for start-up farm businesses, especially for low-income people who would not otherwise have access to land.

Each neighborhood has one or two community gardens for the residents to use. Most of us like to grow some of our own food.

A New Paradigm of Land-Use

In the US, developers typically build one house per acre with lots of roads and garages, using 90% of the land and leaving 10% as natural areas. We wanted to demonstrate that you can build on just 10% and leave 90% of the land for natural areas and farming. We had to get special zoning that allows houses to be only 5 feet apart. Our homes are very tightly clustered and the pedestrian streets create a beautiful park-like setting with fruit trees, picnic tables and children's play space.

The co-housing model is a great way of balancing privacy and community. People have privacy within their homes. When they want a sense of community they just walk out of their door and there are plenty of kids playing and people to interact with. We have community meals for the neighborhood or village 3 times a week, and many parties and celebrations.

We also have several meetings for making decisions together by consensus. There is sharing, camaraderie and, as can be expected, also some conflict. We have had a lot of interest from researchers, from the public, national and international media and students. We are having an influence way beyond anything that I could have imagined back in 1991.

Regional and National Action

We have helped to catalyze a dialogue in the region, mainly through our educational work with colleges and universities. In 2002 we were approached by Ithaca College's professors who asked us to write a grant application with them, to teach courses on 'the science of sustainability'. Together we received a National Science Foundation grant, which helped fund our educational work for 3 years. It was a huge learning experience both for Ithaca College and for EcoVillage Ithaca.

In ecology there is something known as the 'edge effect'; that's when two ecosystems come together such as the ocean and the shore, or the forest and the field. It is in this intersection that most species live and most biological action takes place, and that's how we felt in our interactions with Ithaca College. We, as grassroots activists, were stimulating Ithaca College to think very differently about their programs and helping their students to actively participate in sustainability practices. It also helped our residents to get better at teaching and to learn more about how to work with young people. It was a profound mutual learning. The college even got a national award for cutting edge sustainability programs.

With the new paradigm of land-use, 90% of the land is saved for nature.

153

Cooperating With Urban Planners

We had had 20 years of creating and caring for EcoVillage Ithaca and we wondered whether there was a way to pass on what we had learnt to other ecovillage developers around the country. To this end, we were invited by the Tompkins County Planning Department to partner with them in asking for a grant from the US Environmental Protection Agency (EPA) to promote our ideas as a Climate Showcase Community. We received the grant, and this has funded our educational work for almost 4 years.

It has been a fascinating process, working with planners, local architects and builders. Our third neighborhood here at the EcoVillage is called TREE — Third Residential EcoVillage Experience, with extremely energy efficient homes, some at the German Passive House standard. There are only 84 of these buildings in the whole of the US and 7 of those are in our third neighborhood. Some of the homes are at Net Zero, producing more energy than they use. In our cold climate that's really something, and we showed that it doesn't cost much more than standard construction methods.

We are part of a countywide effort to try to reduce greenhouse gas emissions by 80% by the year 2050. In the US that is radical! TREE homes demonstrate that a well-built house with solar panels can reduce greenhouse gas emissions by 93-100% compared to other homes in the county. The Planning Department is taking that seriously and figuring out what laws need to be changed to promote this kind of development.

Sustainability in Practice

We continue trying to unravel next steps on how to take this way of living and expand it to more places, to people of different income ranges, and to different locations including the city, country and the edge of cities. When I say "we", I mean the project team of county planners, architects and builders. Five of us have worked very closely together for the last 3 years and spoken at many conferences around the country. This model is different enough to be interesting, but not too threatening. It is fascinating to see how change can happen when people get excited about the principles and the values and see that there are real examples of people living this way. So they know it can be done and that gives them momentum to try it in their communities. They won't necessarily try everything, but they might experiment. It's another example of the 'edge effect'. There is a great deal of aliveness in this intersection between local government, local business, and grassroots groups like our ecovillage. A lot can be learnt from one another!

It's a real privilege to live in a close-knit community like ours. It's not always easy; there are 240 people of all ages and everyone has an opinion. But this way of life builds in great resilience — we learn to listen to each other and respect those that have the most practical suggestions. And we inspire each other to learn new things all the time. It's a very dynamic place to live and learn.

Keywords for Solution Library:
Densely Clustered Housing — living closely together in order to leave more natural spaces
Co-housing Village — augmenting private homes with shared community facilities
CSA Farming — creating supportive relationships between growers and consumers of agricultural products
solution.ecovillage.org

Four Decades On

The Farm / Tennessee, USA

In 1971, a caravan of 60 brightly painted school buses and an assortment of other vehicles carrying more than 300 hippie idealists landed on an abandoned farm in central Tennessee. They had a mission: to be part of something bigger than themselves, to follow a peaceful and spiritual path, and to make a difference in the world. Albert Bates, a former environmental rights lawyer, has lived at The Farm for the past 40 years. He became a co-recipient of the Right Livelihood Award for his work with The Farm's relief and development agency, Plenty International. He also served as President of GEN for several years.

Albert Bates

Albert Bates

The year I left my parents' home and ventured out into the world, Bob Dylan released his *Bringing It All Back Home* album, singing about the hypocrisies of our all-enveloping consumer civilization, making an appeal to throw sand in the gears and to choose something better. "Don't go along," he sang, "I mean no harm nor put fault / On anyone that lives in a vault / But it's alright, Ma, if I can't please him."

For me, like millions in the post-war Baby Boom, it was good advice. We were not our parents' generation, those described by President Kennedy as tempered by war and disciplined by a hard and bitter peace. We were a generation that came of age in peacetime, to the beat of rock 'n' roll and surf music. We challenged racial inequality and stood for women's' rights. Behind our parents' backs we sampled the liberation of 'The Pill' and the forbidden fruits of psychedelic sacraments. We were not inclined towards aggregations of material possessions or dominance over nature. We marched for peace, honesty and justice; left our universities and the allure of white-collar jobs to become nomads; questioned everything and everyone. They called us 'hippies', a word that came from jazz — 'hip' was brought to this country though the West African Wolof language word 'hepicat', which means 'one who has his eyes open'.

What are Hippies?

In a 1986 interview in *The Sun*, The Farm's founder, Stephen Gaskin, said, "You've got to be a rich country to have hippies. They're a free, privileged scholar class that can study what they want. They're like young princelings. It's really been an upscale movement, in a way, except for when it

Photo: Alberto Ruz

broke through. And when it broke through was when it was the most revolutionary and really scared the Establishment, because hippies bond across cultural, religious, and class lines."

Ronald Reagan described a hippie as a person who "dresses like Tarzan, has hair like Jane, and smells like Cheeta". Even today popular culture stereotypes hippies as long-haired, unwashed, unkempt drug users with leftist political leanings.

Those who moved to The Farm did so because of shared values and visions. They wanted common land that was jointly owned and managed, where they could live together, through mutual support, and live off the energy flows (soil, sun, water, animal cycles) nature provided. They wanted a place where they could build and sustain a village economy; where people exchanged basic goods and services with each other and the surrounding region. These are not lofty goals, until you place them against the background of rapid climate change, energy descent, a debt-based economic system breaching biophysical and ethical limits, and a militaristic national security state that is beginning to resemble Germany in 1933, except with weapons that were only in the pages of science fiction magazines back then.

156

In 1971, a caravan of 60 school buses with more than 300 hippie idealists took off to found one of the first ecovillages.

A Tight-knit Community

Our idea of a close-knit community is one where any child can reach for an adult's hand without being concerned which adult it is. If one neighbor has a dispute with another, it does not come to an angry exchange, but is resolved rationally, whether through mutual respect or amicable mediation by friends. No-one need fear loss of support, loss of friendship, or sudden calamity because within these borders there is this web of kinship, the invisible glue that binds us, that is strong and resilient.

The Farm was determined to work the intricacies of the national legal and tax systems not by dodging inspectors but by meeting or exceeding every code requirement. Its small alternative school received no support from the state or local government but today has grown to be a hub for home school networks in the region, with an enrollment of over 1,000 students per year. The clinic and dispensary, whose midwives were considered outlaws at first, provide a standard of care in many ways superior to the national medical system, with its own licensed physician assistants, paramedics, and midwives. We have an ecology of businesses which use virtually every type of organizational structure and we now sell many of our products — electronic instruments, tempeh and mushroom starter kits, books and new media — beyond our bioregion, into the global marketplace.

A Cooler Place

In the early days we soldered solar cells onto metal cookie baking sheets to make enough power to hear our own music on our own low power community radio station. Today we are selling power to the national grid whenever the sun shines. Our biochar — from bamboo kilns, keylined fields and hardwood forests — net sequesters 5 times the greenhouse gas footprint of all our residences, businesses and visitors each year. The Farm is a cool place, one that cools the planet.

Whether you are studying the origins of personal computers and the internet, are a cancer patient grateful for medical marijuana, or are a concerned environmentalist thinking about what needs to happen in the next decades if we are to survive on a hot, crowded planet, you have to admit the hippies were right. They were right about peace, love, solar energy, civil rights, free speech, meditation, yoga, homebrew computers and backyard organic gardens. The hippies did more than make great music; they pioneered bioregionalism, permaculture and ecovillages.

The Farm is one of the better known icons of the 1960s' hippie culture. We are now four decades on the land and four generations. The first generation was not the 320 flower-children that arrived in Tennessee from San Francisco in painted schoolbuses and VW vans, but their parents, who began trickling in 10 years later when they saw what a good thing their kids had going.

The second generation, the pioneers, gave birth to a third generation in the back of blocked-up buses, homespun yurts, rough-hewn shacks and tar-papered geodesic domes. Those children then gave birth to a fourth generation, children born to the children born to the land and to the guiding philosophy, often with assistance from the same midwives who coached their grandmothers.

In all of the non-violent revolutions around the world today there are common goals that are not difficult to comprehend or appreciate. In each case there is a desire to create a new society. If the change were to be accomplished with violence, it would become a mostly futile gesture; "moving the furniture around," as Stephen Gaskin often said. Accomplished without violence, the act of birth can express the greater devotion to higher values we wish to instill.

The legacy the hippies gave The Farm, and the larger culture, was this: Stephen, who passed away in 2014, used to say, "there is no Farm," meaning it's important to remember to "keep it in your mind and not forget/that it is not he or she or them or it/you belong to" (Bob Dylan). You're not part of anything or anyone and nobody owns you. You are you. Now do something with it.

Challenges We Face Today

On a cold winter's day some hundred voting members take refuge from
the freezing rain to gather in the Farm's Community Center to attend our
Quarterly Meeting. Looking past reports by the membership committee,
housing committee, water manager and others, I can see where our tensions
and challenges inevitably arise. We've had another jump in property
tax, something we can expect to see more of as Washington's military
adventurism bleeds resources from the periphery to the centre.

One of the homes of The Farm.

For us, the taxes raise a barrier to young people, who often come to us
already shouldering debt burdens from student loans and a lack of medical
insurance. We don't like to turn them away, but the reality is if they cannot
find a paying job in our rural location, they won't be able to pay the
monthly assessments we ask of all Farm residents. There are few jobs to
be found this far from a metropolitan area, and starting a business implies
having a market to sell into, something that may be quite some distance
away.

The problem is no less acute for children born and raised here. After
school they need a place to work, and since we dropped our communal
form of economics in 1984, that means looking for a job the same way
a newcomer would. Sometimes there is a friend or relative within the
community that is able to hire them, but more often they end up working at
a supermarket or business in a nearby town, or taking their college degree

to find a professional position in a distant city. These are troubling trends, and as yet we have not come up with any good answers. We are hoping for more young entrepreneurs, but we can't support them to get started and it is very rare for our local banks to support them either.

I have no regrets about my youthful decision to chuck a promising career as a Manhattan attorney and pick up a hoe. I would not choose differently even if I could travel back four decades and decide again. But today there is a new generation, born in this century, tempered and empowered by new forms of communication that completely envelop and consume them, disciplined by an unforgiving reckoning with limits to growth, the profligate waste of a one-time inheritance of fossil sunlight, and the spoils their predecessors made of the atmosphere, oceans, rainforests and original instructions.

For the next generation, and the one after it, and the one after that, the world will be a vastly different place than it was for me. When I show someone how to make biochar, brew compost tea or lay a keyline across a valley, I am showing them what they can do that will be different and that might just give their children something better. When people come to my village and see our process of consensus, our reverence for the sacred, our healthy diet and unwavering devotion to social activism in the greater world, we hope they still become inspired to do something similar.

Ecovillages arise from a concatenation of causes, but first among them is hope for the future and a willingness to act to make that real.

www.thefarm.org

Keywords for Solution Library:
Biochar from Bamboo kilns — sequestering CO_2 while rebuilding humus layers
Keyline Fields — harvesting rainwater following contour lines
Compost Tea — producing liquid manure from organic waste
solution.ecovillage.org

Getting to the Source

The Source / Jamaica

The Source — Farm, Foundation and Learning Village — is a multicultural, intergenerational ecovillage, located in Johns Town in the parish of St. Thomas, Jamaica. Its ecological mission and vision is to respect natural life, its systems and processes — preserving wildlife and botanical habitat, and creating a lifestyle that regenerates rather than diminishes the integrity of the source farm environment. Nicola Shirley-Phillips, 47, is one of the founders.

Photo: Nicola Shirley-Phillips

Ecovillage life is a healthy way to grow up.

Nicola Shirley-Phillips

How do I tell the story of The Source? There is a politically correct story we tell our visitors and this is what you will find on our website. However, the deeper story is full of magic. If you want a 'cleaner' version you can visit our website. If you want to hear what really happened, read on.

I feel that The Source started before my birth, before my mother's birth and her mother's. Each generation and each experience is the building block of the sum of our reality. I guess I need to start somewhere in this continuum. So I will start with a consultation by a traditional African Akan priest in Philadelphia. Here I was, very nervous, a Jamaican and Catholic, doing something that was taboo in my circles.

The session turned my world upside down. Most importantly, I was told that I would be part of a group starting a village, and that I would be living in that village by 2010. This consultation happened in September 1999. After that meeting, I went home, had a good cry and promptly forgot about the whole thing; it was too crazy and out of my realm of understanding.

Jamaica Returns...

I lived in Philadelphia, owned 2 busy restaurants and had no clue about villages or intentional communities. For the next 5 years, I catered for and managed the restaurants and built up a number of development projects in the larger community. All the while, I was feeling unfulfilled. During this period, I started to have many dreams.

My mother had three children and moved us to the United States when she divorced our father. All three of her children graduated from schools in the US with Bachelor and Masters degrees and, as they say in Jamaica, 'threw a stone behind us' — meaning we had no intention of going back to Jamaica except for vacations. However, my outlook on life began to change. When I met a group of Jamaican professors in Philadelphia whose mission it was to develop service learning projects in Jamaica, I joined them and started to bring groups of students to Jamaica, more specifically to the parish of St. Thomas.

St. Thomas is the neighboring parish to Kingston, the capital of Jamaica. It is well known for the Rebellion of 1865 and has never recovered from the fact that the newly emancipated Africans dared to stand up to the British Crown. Since that time, it has been continually overlooked and underrepresented in terms of educational, financial and social welfare for its citizens. On one of these trips to St. Thomas, my mother mentioned to a friend that she was looking for 3-6 acres of land. Upon our return to the US, the friend called us and told us of a 63 acre property with a stream, small storage structure and stone water tank. My mother convinced me to fly back and take a look. The land was all she was dreaming of and we could just afford the price if we all contributed. Mom put down a deposit and got a mortgage; we all split the mortgage and paid it monthly. (The mortgage is now paid off.)

During this time, I was having more powerful dreams, luring me back to Jamaica. The ancestors were working hard. I was also at a point in my life when I was sick of the restaurant business. The restaurant had been depicted in a bestselling book, *In Her Shoes,* which had been turned into a Twentieth Century Fox Production starring Cameron Diaz, Tony Collette and Shirley Maclaine. My small oasis had turned into a hugely successful, hip spot that I wanted to run away from. However, my dreams told me that I could not yet leave. There was something else for me to do in the US. I was encouraged to get my Masters degree in Community Economic Development. I listened and took on the challenge.

Sometimes I can be very dense! Buying 63 acres of land did not remind me of my consultation with the Akan priest and the message about starting a village. It was only when coming back to Jamaica and working to establish a Sewing Cooperative for Teen Mothers for my Master's thesis that it dawned on me. Each time I went to Jamaica, I took someone along. I would visit the land to ensure that all was well. Each friend who accompanied me shared their wish to stay: there are breathtaking views of the Caribbean Sea and lush foliage. After many such conversations we realized that we were being asked to create a village. We had no idea what it meant or how to do this. A family friend had been to a few 'intentional communities for natural building' workshops and retreats; he mentioned words like ecovillage, sustainable living, natural building and ecological stewardship. We learned that a subculture had been growing for years that could provide us with guidelines, books, workshops and consultants. We all got busy doing research, going on site visits to various intentional communities and looking at best practices and models.

Earthaven's Contribution

In 2006, we visited Earthaven in North Carolina and met Diana Leafe Christian, who authored 2 books and tons of articles on intentional communities. We read the books and took in all the information we could find. We began meetings with our interested friends, and very soon we came up against challenges because people could not see how they could afford to move to Jamaica and build a new life there. We invited Diana to help us navigate these challenges and assist us with specific action-steps to create structure and harmony in moving forward. She also recommended that we bring a permaculturist to help us map and design the village. Chuck Marsh, a founding member of Earthaven was selected. He visited, fell in love with Jamaica and is currently a member of The Source. Once we had our permaculture design and formal consensus process in place, and with ongoing assistance from the ancestors, we embarked upon creating The Source Farm Foundation and Ecovillage.

Photo: Nicola Shirley-Phillips

Everybody is helping to build the green houses of The Source.

The Source's Magic

I have been telling this story through my eyes and my experience. I can tell you that The Source has saved my life. Everything I have ever wanted to do is right here in this project on the land. Vision, energy and creative potential abound in this place. People are inspired, electrified and moved to action. The ancestors have allowed us to create a canvas for others to paint on and develop their mission and vision for their life.

My mother and siblings can tell their own story about how The Source saved them. My brother became unemployed after the 2008 housing crash. He decided to move his family to Jamaica and is now our resident farmer on the land. He got his degree in Education and Design but always had a love of farming. Now, he's finally able to support his family and pursue his passion.

People come to visit us and never want to leave. This is what The Source does. The land holds them and the spirit of the land nurtures them. People who come to this demonstration village learn so much and are amazed that we, as a network of extended family and friends, can work and live together. We have created community kitchens, a nature school, off-the-grid living, an organic farm, the natural dye collective with local community women, a Farmers Market in Kingston, the Taino Camp, a Summer Literacy and Art Program, a Sunday Dinner Project, the Jamaica Sustainable Farm Enterprise Program (that just got funded by USAID) and many community development projects within St. Thomas. This work is daunting and we enjoy every minute of it.

165

Earthbag Houses are a cheap and ecological way to build.

Photo: Nicola Shirley-Phillips

Core of the Community

In this moment, our core group consists of 13 families. Each family has their own home using earthbag construction. We all have a community kitchen and pool our resources to hire a part-time cook. We eat together, but not for every meal. We use formal consensus as decision-making and the I Ching to help us. We have monthly work parties, we assist on the farm and we support each other to be creatively involved in projects that are overlapping. We have a community school and each person teaches 1-2 hours weekly.

Here are some of the lessons that we have already learnt:

- Feel free to say 'no' to potential new members.
- The immediate community may take a while to warm up and understand what you are doing. Keep focussed.
- Keep to your community agreements.
- Ensure that people are **In Love** with the concept of living together, for you will need this energy to weather the storms.
- Try out the best practices that are available to you — experience is the best teacher.
- Design, Design and Redesign.
- Spend money on a professional who understands land planning — it will save you in the long run.
- Remember not to take things too seriously.
- Always honor the folks that came before you and remember there is a lot of unemployment in the spirit world — you can put them to work on your behalf.

As we are a young community, over the past 8 years we have been listening and learning. For Jamaicans and people of African descent, first emerging from slavery and then from an enslaving system, working and living together in community is a huge thing. Demonstrating that we can do this and pool our resources is what many people are amazed at. We've worked through challenges together. We have been blessed in having some of the best consultants and experts to guide us. Many people come to The Source and marvel at the infrastructure that we've built, but often don't notice the inner work and interpersonal aspects that make this possible. We choose to work for a larger purpose. We are a young community, ever evolving and co-creating. We can't wait to see how The Source is developed by the next generation. I have learned to listen and have faith, work the edges and trust in the ancestors.

Keywords for Solution Library:

Community Schools — allowing children to learn within their social environment

Earth Bag Houses — building low-cost housing from local materials

solution.ecovillage.org

Ordinary People Doing Extraordinary Things

Earthaven Ecovillage / Southern Appalachians, USA

Earthaven is an aspiring ecovillage in a mountain forest setting near Asheville, North Carolina. It is dedicated to caring for people and the Earth by learning, living, and demonstrating a holistic, sustainable culture. "We're just ordinary people, trying to do extraordinary things", said Earthaven cofounder Chuck Marsh. Diana Leafe Christian is a long-term member.

Diana Leafe Christian

Diana Leafe Christian

I joined Earthaven Ecovillage in western North Carolina because of the beauty of its mountain forest setting, its ecovillage vision and its people. At Earthaven we live in passive-solar, earth-plastered dwellings with solar panels for electricity and metal roofs for roof-water catchment. Everyone has composting toilets. We offer workshops on permaculture design, natural building, and other aspects of ecological and social sustainability. Walking through the forest, people who take our tours see dappled sunlight and ferns on the forest floor, and hear birdsong, frogs and the babbling of streams. Unlike most parts of the eastern US, we have abundant water and abundant sunlight. To me, it's paradise.

I'm especially interested in how people successfully start new ecovillages, and how they resolve conflicts that can arise when people have widely different assumptions about the purpose of their community and even appear to be in different paradigms about it. So I'll describe Earthaven's founding, the differences over the years between its older and younger members, and how its younger members have taken the initiative to resolve these in ways that give me hope.

Earthaven's Beginnings

Earthaven began in 1994 when 18 founders, including three permaculture designers, bought 320 acres in the mountains. After doing a topographical survey and exploring the property, they created a permaculture-based Site Plan, including future agriculture fields and orchards, a village centre, residential neighborhoods on gentle south-facing slopes, sacred sites, bridges and roads. They then began clearing forest and building roads.

The group was vulnerable to foreclosure by the owner-financers — losing the property if they didn't have enough new members with joining fees each year to make the mortgage payments. So they borrowed money from members, friends, and neighbors to create the 'Earthshares Fund', which they used to pay the mortgage when they didn't have enough money from the joining fees. In 2004 Earthaven paid off the owner-financers; and in 2006 paid off the Earthshares' lenders.

In our early years the two other challenges were the lack of homes — people lived in tents, canvas yurts, and camper shells — and the lack of onsite jobs. To address these problems, in the late 1990s several young men began the Forestry Co-op, a cooperatively owned business practising sustainable forestry, sustainable saw-milling, and building passive-solar homes for members. They borrowed money and bought chainsaws, a portable sawmill and carpentry tools. They taught themselves forestry, saw-milling and building construction; and paying themselves barely minimum wages, they leapt into this new field to meet our needs for jobs and housing. One often heard the sounds of chainsaws, sawmills, table saws and power hammers, as serious home-building was continuously underway in at least one or more neighborhoods. However, despite the many homes that they built over the years, the Forestry Co-op struggled financially. After six and a half years of barely breaking even and sometimes going for weeks with no pay, they disbanded the business. While this was sad for many, it also resulted in several young members having solid income-earning skills, from carpentry and home-building to electrical work, off-grid solar design and installation, water and propane plumbing, and sustainable forestry.

Photo: Diana Leafe Christian

169

*Andy Bosley and Julie McMahon of Yellowroot Farm,
a biodynamic CSA farm at Earthaven.*

Differing Interests

My mom and I began visiting regularly in late 2000, became members in 2002, and built a small house and moved onsite in 2003. I soon joined the Membership and Promotions committees. One of my first tasks was to help revise Earthaven's website so that it provided the practical information visitors and potential members needed to know.

In most ecovillages and intentional communities, people show neighborly generosity and affection. However, in the early 2000s there were tensions between younger and older members about the place of children. The founders and earliest members had originally discouraged people with small children because they wanted new members with enough free time to physically build the village, and also there was no safe way to deal with diapers without polluting the streams. As more and more young people joined and wanted to begin families, they, and many visitors, reported feeling a distinct 'anti-family vibe' at Earthaven. It was so discouraging some young people left the community. So, several newer younger members and I wrote what we called 'Family Friendly' proposals to make the community easier for and more welcoming to families with young children.

These proposals passed after much discussion and negotiation. Nowadays we have many exuberant toddlers as well as a few older children and young teens.

Living together with people and plants: One of Earthhaven´s green houses.

Other differences involved Earthaven's meeting culture and decision-making. For example, most founders were spiritually and ecologically oriented childless people in their late 40s when they bought the land. They and our early members were a tight, emotionally connected group who valued spiritual practice, their heartfelt visionary ideals and deep emotional sharing of personal issues in business meetings. Several members told me this was how they felt connected to one another. Meetings were often characterized by strong emotions, including expressing affection and caring, crying, laughing and sometimes shouting. Yet many younger members have been put off by this meeting culture. Many told me that they didn't want to participate in meetings with people their parents' (or grandparents') age who express strong emotions when disagreeing on proposals. Instead, the younger members wanted shorter meetings that focused on taking the next steps and getting on with the process of building the village and helping us meet our ecovillage goals. They say that strong emotional expression does not make them feel connected to others. Rather, what makes them feel connected and bonded is a shared sense of accomplishment in working toward and achieving community goals, as well as social activities outside of meetings. They like connection in a positive, high-energy way — that happy feeling of 'We're doing it!'

Decision-Making in Earthaven

Also, until relatively recently Earthaven used the form of consensus which I call 'consensus-with-unanimity', meaning anyone could block a proposal for any reason, with no recourse. One of our more controversial topics has been agriculture; our young farmers and several older members strongly disagreed about how many fields we should clear and lease to members for small farms, and the way in which forest should be sustained. So when younger members leased and cleared land for their first few farms in the mid-2000s, several older members were appalled because the clearing process and the agricultural practices didn't meet their interpretation of Earthaven's standards for ecological rigor. The farmers had interpreted Earthaven's standards differently and thought they had met them. So when discussing proposals, especially about future agriculture, our meetings often became tense because we all expected someone to block a positive decision, and sometimes a few older members did. Between 2007 and 2010 new agriculture at Earthaven was severely slowed down.

These years were difficult. Because of the way several older members behaved in meetings and the consensus process that allowed blocking with no recourse, young people and a few of us older ones became discouraged and demoralized. Eventually the younger members stopped going to business meetings entirely. Several left the community.

But there was hope. Led by one of our young farmers, for seven years some of us explored alternative ways to use consensus and deal with what is sometimes called the 'tyranny of the minority'. Between 2012 and 2014 Earthaven cautiously proposed and approved two incremental changes to our consensus process, designed to allow us to move forward more effectively in meeting our ecovillage goals. In mid-2014 we changed it a third time — radically. We still discuss and modify proposals, but instead of calling for consensus, we vote. If 85% or more say Yes to a proposal, it passes; if less than 50% say Yes, it doesn't. If between 50% and 85% say 'Yes', we hold a series of meetings between a few members who said 'Yes' and a few who said 'No', in order to create a new proposal addressing the same issues. If that's not possible, the first proposal comes back for a 66% percent supermajority vote. Although a few grieved the loss of the form of consensus they loved, this last change has made a huge difference in community well-being.

171

Moving Forward

Our young people have consistently behaved in ways that convince me of their consciousness, confidence, leadership and integrity. Now, in 2015, it seems our generations have come together again. Two younger members are raising money through loans from older members and friends to buy out the buildings and infrastructure of two departing members: one young member wants to revive a dormant small farm, and the other wants to create a cottage industry offering onsite lodging and dining for visitors. Younger and older members raised the money for a shared off-grid renewable power system which will improve the amount and reliability of electricity in their neighborhood. And several young parents have created two shared childcare and home-schooling programs for members' and neighbors' children.

Earthaven Ecovillage couldn't have existed and continued without the energy, vision, and motivation of its older members who founded the project, designed its permaculture-based site plan and innovated its EarthShares Fund. And we couldn't have moved forward with more ease and grace in governance, in built homes, in creating small farms and starting up new cottage industries and social enterprises without the vision, energy, drive and confidence of our young people. Now Earthaven is thriving again. Visitors love our Saturday tours and sustainability workshops. We're doing what we intended all along — living meaningful lives in the good company of friends, and helping educate, encourage and inspire the mainstream however we can. Visitors come here, learn from what we're doing, and discover that they, too, might become 'ordinary people doing extraordinary things'.

www.earthaven.org

Keywords for Solution Library:
Consensus Decision Making — listening to all the voices
Sociocracy — using consent-based decision making inter-linking circles
solution.ecovillage.org

ASIA

Ecovillages... In Our DNA

Ladakh / India

Helena Norberg-Hodge has been working in Ladakh for the past 40 years. She is currently working with 80 villages to protect and support their chosen pathways to sustainability. While these villages have been ecologically sustainable for many centuries, today they need to consciously treasure their cultural heritage and combine traditional and innovative solutions to ensure social and economic survival. In order to do that they are adapting ecovillage strategies. Helena Norberg-Hodge is deeply connected to the localisation movement, and is a founding member of GEN and recipient of the Right Livelihood Award.

Photo: Claire Leimbach

Helena Norberg-Hodge

Helena Norberg-Hodge

Falling in Love with Ladakh

I have had my eyes opened to the profound importance of ecovillages in Ladakh or 'Little Tibet', where I have spent much of my time over the last forty years. It was there that I came to know first-hand the people living in nature-based communities and experienced how their deep connection to the earth and to others provided them with an extended, inclusive sense of self. In this culture, there seemed to be no need to retreat behind boundaries of fear and self-protection.

I first arrived here in 1975 as part of a documentary film team when the area was thrown open to 'development' and tourism. I was intending to spend just 6 weeks before returning to my work as a linguist in Paris. However, the Ladakhis' irrepressible joy and contagious laughter captivated me and I decided to stay on to work on the language after the film was finished.

Over the following years, I witnessed dramatic changes that came about as the region was opened up to 'growth and development'. Ladakh was being submerged in an avalanche of imported consumer goods, tourism, westernised schooling, new polluting technologies—including DDT and asbestos. And all the while people were subjected to media images of a romanticised urban consumer culture that painted them as backward and primitive. I saw young people who previously had deep self-respect become confused and demoralised. For young boys the new role model was Rambo and for the girls Barbie dolls. Unemployment, self-rejection, poverty and pollution became commonplace. Community bonds were eroded as people competed for scarce jobs in the new, urban, money economy. In 1989, the psychological and economic pressures culminated in violent conflict between Buddhists and Muslims.

Healthy Sources of Energy

As the negative changes escalated in Ladakh, I became even more motivated to do what I could to present alternatives to a development path that was, so clearly, socially and environmentally destructive. First of all, it was clear that the urbanising development in Ladakh was based on fossil fuels. The government subsidised the use of coal, diesel and kerosene and people were starting to use them to heat their homes in winter. However, Ladakh, lying high on the Tibetan plateau and with more than 300 days of sunshine a year, was ideally suited to the use of solar energy. There was also plenty of scope for using hydro power.

So, I began writing letters to the Indian government, pleading for policies that would build on the strengths of the traditional culture and promote the use of renewable energy. And we began a 'Trombe wall' project. This elegantly simple solar technology for heating houses proved to be ideally suited to Ladakh and was easily adapted to the traditional architecture and available materials. A black-painted, south-facing, mud-brick wall absorbs and stores solar energy; and the rays of the low winter sun effectively heat the room, while those of the high summer sun barely touch the wall, keeping the room cool and comfortable.

Building a Trombe Wall, a solar efficient wall, using simple means.

Ladakh Ecological Development Group

These activities attracted the interest of some of Ladakh's spiritual and political leaders. We launched the Ladakh Ecological Development Group (LEDeG) together in 1983, to demonstrate a whole range of appropriate technologies. These included solar ovens, water heaters, greenhouses (which lengthened the growing season by 6 months!), micro-hydroelectricity installations and the amazing 'ram pump' (made by our own technical staff entirely from standard plumbing parts), using gravity instead of imported petroleum to pump water.

LEDeG became the most influential non-governmental organisation in the region. Indira Gandhi inaugurated our Ecology Centre in 1984 and this was consecrated by His Holiness the Dalai Lama. We ended up working in about 80 villages throughout the whole region.

In addition to renewable energy, we developed an organic agriculture programme. However, it's important to point out that whether in energy or in agriculture, we were not trying to tell the Ladakhis how to develop — rather, we were demonstrating alternatives to conventional development. It was clear that people had almost no information about the materials and changes that were being pushed on them by outside 'experts'. People knew nothing about the environmental movement in the West or the problems and side-effects of everything from fossil fuels and hybrid seeds to artificial fertilisers and pesticides like DDT.

The Ladakhis were not only ignorant about our ecological problems in the West. But as in the rest of the so-called 'developing' world, the message coming through conventional development, advertising and media was that the West was some kind of paradise. It appeared as though we had lives of constant leisure and incredible wealth. People literally thought that we did no work!

Reality Tours

We carried out a whole range of educational efforts to counter these ideas — through community meetings, radio programmes, theatre and workshops in Ladakh. We also organized 'Reality Tours', sponsoring community leaders to experience the West for themselves. In this work, GEN was of central importance. We were able to highlight examples of people who had come to realise the emptiness and destructive nature of the urban consumer culture. The Ladakhis could hear from people about our spiritual, psychological, ecological and economic problems. Importantly, through GEN they could also learn that people were creating more meaningful and sustainable ways of living. The deeper dialogue between Westerners and Ladakhis led to the recognition that Ladakh, like other traditional, land-based communities, had a lot to offer these Western movements. This in turn helped young Ladakhis regain greater respect for their culture.

Not all of these activities were met with appreciation. From the very beginning, Indian government officials were convinced that I was a CIA agent and warned Ladakhi leaders not to join our efforts. So my husband John Page (who had joined me after 3 years) and I were under constant surveillance for many years. Another difficult phase was a period in the 1980s when young Ladakhi men, in particular, were actively opposed to our work. They had become sold on the Rambo/fossil fuel path and decided that we were not only wasting time with our renewable energy projects but probably pocketing millions in the process. Over the years, the most challenging problem has been the fact that, despite all our efforts, conventional development has continued to increase both pollution and unemployment.

Nevertheless, I'm happy to report that for the last two decades support from the Ladakhis has continued to increase, and despite the unemployment pressures, relations between Buddhists and Muslims have remained peaceful. Most importantly, leaders from our ecology group set up a semi-independent government, with virtually identical goals to those of LEDeG.

Ecovillages are in our DNA

Over the years I came to realise that the Ladakhis' joy and dignity arose from their deep sense of connection with one another and with the Earth, and that this is how we have evolved for most of human history. In fact, ecovillages must be in our DNA! This is why people from all around the world, who have experienced urban or suburban life, cut off from others and from nature, develop a yearning to rebuild their spiritual connections to life.

It also became clear to me that these spiritual connections were anchored in local economic interactions. Communities were built on economic ties that fostered a daily experience of interdependence with others and with nature. This, in turn, provided a healthy foundation for individuals to grow and be nurtured, to feel that they belonged — to a people, a culture and their place on earth.

In consumer society, our connections to each other and to the rest of nature have been largely severed. Large bureaucracies or businesses mediate almost all our interactions. In this way, we become dependent on institutions rather than one another. For example, many middlemen and hundreds, if not thousands, of miles, separate the majority of us from the source of our food.

177

As I became increasingly aware of the importance of maintaining or rebuilding our local economic structures, I started speaking about my activities and writing about the importance of shifting away from dependence on a distant global economy, and promoted 'decentralisation' or 'localisation' as a systemic alternative.

This led to the setting up of a small international organisation called the Ladakh Project. In 1991, this seed grew into the International Society for Ecology and Culture, which has recently been renamed 'Local Futures'. Over the years, we have made films, organised conferences and lectures, written books and articles, and led workshops on the multiple benefits of localisation. At the same time we have been providing information about the systemic effects of the global economy: from rising CO_2 emissions to other forms of pollution, from poverty and unemployment to an epidemic of fear and depression.

Much of our work over the past four decades has been about deepening a dialogue between the global North and global South. As economic 'development' sweeps across the planet, schoolbooks as well as blaring television commercials carry the message that more traditional, indigenous ways of life are inferior. Westerners have an important role to play in countering these myths, by showing how we are seeking to regain the connectedness that people in less industrialised cultures have not yet completely lost. Sharing experiences across the world can help us all to make more informed choices and to build a powerful people's movement for fundamental change. As part of this work, we are now spearheading the formation of the International Alliance for Localisation (IAL).

Helena with elder women of Ladakh, who strive together to maintain the culture of happiness and sustainability

Ancient Futures and the Economics of Happiness

The story of Ladakh has spread far and wide through my book, *Ancient Futures*. I wrote it after 16 years of witnessing change, and a few years later we made a film of the same title. Both film and book have now been translated into over 40 languages. Our later film 'The Economics of Happiness' expands the theme of *Ancient Futures* to show that communities all around the world are beginning to demonstrate the multiple spiritual, social, ecological and even economic benefits of localisation. The 'Economics of Happiness' has also been translated into multiple languages and has become something of a movement in itself! In tiny, far flung villages from Japan and Korea to Peru and Chile, small groups huddle in cafés or homes around a laptop — while huge audiences in lecture halls and conferences in the capital cities of the world hear the story and are inspired to take meaningful action. The unprecedented reach has continued to amaze us and it seems that the core message of our work is starting to achieve a critical mass.

www.localfutures.org

Keywords for Solution Library:

Localisation — promoting the renewal of local communities, economies and cultures
Trombe Wall — using passive solar building techniques
Index of Happiness — measuring well-being as an alternative concept of wealth
solution.ecovillage.org

179

Ecovillage and Decolonisation

Wongsanit Ashram / Bangkok, Thailand

Pracha is a founder and Narumon a longtime member of Wongsanit Ashram, a long-term member of the Global Ecovillage Network. Both are active in a social activism movement that shares ecovillage awareness and practices all over South East Asia.

Narumon Paiboonsittikun

My country is changing very fast. In Asian society, we are expected to be calm and polite, and not to show our negative feelings. This leads to the situation that we don't really know who we are. We lack the ability to take decisions freely. Resulting inner tensions can explode into violence. Many of my generation are volunteering for NGOs and go to communities and Ashrams for a while in order to explore other values and ways of being. In 2000, I came to the Wongsanit Ashram. At first, I thought it was a dream. I stayed for 5 years, learning about grassroots democracy. It raised a deep doubt in me: Are we really living in a democracy in Thailand? I found that 35 people, who have learnt how to really rule their community in a truthful way, could teach politicians a lot about how to rule a whole country.

Pracha Hutanuwatr

Photo: Leila Dregger

For me, 'ecovillage' is a radical idea, leading in the opposite direction of most governments' understanding of 'development'. In my part of the world, in South East Asia, we are facing a new colonisation in the name of modernisation, development and globalisation. At their core all these strategies seem to promote the same set of values: to conquer nature, to compete with each other, to promote individualism and to reduce the commons. And this is our challenge as ecovillage activists.

Southeast Asia is rich with natural resources and has, a long time ago, already manifested what the term 'ecovillage' describes: sustainability, community, fair economy and deep cultural values. In a country like Thailand, after 50 years of adopting an American Way of Life, the concept of ecovillages necessitates a process of decolonisation of ideas and habits. It entails resistance against technocrats and strategies that destroy nature and make the poor poorer. After 50 years of 'development' in Thailand, the villagers own cars and motorcycles, but everybody is in debt.

And now, in Burma, the window of development is just opening. And the multinationals are rushing in, putting pressure on everybody to develop.

Social and Spiritual Activism

My personal path towards ecovillage started in the 1970s while at university. I asked myself: How can I spend my life with more meaning rather than striving for a house and car? I wanted to leave behind the path of the middle class I was born into. I became a Marxist in order to change the world. But after a while I found that Marxism had some weaknesses. One of them was a lack of knowledge about how to change human behaviour from the inside. Instead, I became a Buddhist monk. I had planned to stay for 2 weeks, but ended up spending 11 years in a monastery.

In university I had been part of a group, along with 15 friends and our teacher Sulak Sivaraksa. We were inspired by Gandhi who used ashrams as places of empowerment to help liberate the Indian population from British occupation. When I left monkhood in 1986, my teacher sent me to India to visit Gandhi's ashrams. I travelled from north to south to see the style of the ashrams in their third generation. Some of them really have become agents for social change.

Creating an Ashram of engaged Buddhism

In 1990, a friend of our teacher gave us 10 hectares of land for Wongsanit Ashram, 1.5 hours away from Bangkok. We explored an original and holistic life, cultivating the land, fishing, building and living in simple houses.

We were 40 people and drafted some basic rules for living together according to the Buddhist basic principles. We experimented with ideas on how to live together, how to combine individual spiritual life and how to attain changes in the wider society, following the inspiration of Gandhi's ashram movement in India. A basic principle of the ashram has been from the beginning to combine mental work, physical work and meditation. We still meditate together at least once a week. And we have a labour day once a month, sometimes every week.

We have no television and no fridge in the ashram. In the beginning, we strongly believed in participatory community management, which means reaching every decision in consensus, sharing power, and through these processes growing together. We took all decisions together — whether to accept newcomers or not, whether we would eat together or in families. Today, we still work with consensus in many cases, but we also learnt that

The Wongsanit Ashram combines spiritual practice and social activism.

sometimes it takes too long. Thus, some issues we vote on by majority and we are also happy to use common sense and find compromises.

We are proud of the oasis that we have created on the site. Lots and lots of trees are growing. Wild animals are coming in, birds and snakes. Outside the ashram they are hunted and killed, but here they know that they can live.

Once you run a project, it needs all your attention and you need to keep finding balance. In 1992, I created a Center for Activism for Social Change as an institution within the framework of the ashram, to support community empowerment all over South East Asia. I was its director for 10 years. It has become our connection with the social movement, combining meditation and social action. Walking side by side, any action can be spiritual. We started this, and a lot of activists joined us. We became part of a paradigm shift all over the country. Although I no longer live at the ashram I endeavour to embody the values in my life and keep up regular contact.

Working in Burma

When I got married to Jane Rasbash, a colleague from the ecovillage of Findhorn, we initiated the Grassroots Leadership Training Programme (GLT) in Myanmar and later got involved with Ecovillage Design Education (EDE) courses and ecovillages. In 1994 we were invited to Burma by villagers who wanted to start a NGO. Burma at that time was an intense experience. The villages had no electricity, we saw many guns in the streets and the people had a very little freedom. But there was much self-sufficiency and a strong connection between leaders and young people. Traditions were still very much alive.. Every time we left Burma, it was a relief. However, we continued to work there for more than 10 years, giving GLT/EDE courses and trainings. Now the projects have grown into a huge NGO network, run by our local friends.

We always use five elements in our training: first, critical understanding of the global situation and the forces that come into and shape our regions. Secondly, we share knowledge about ecology and the environmental situation. Thirdly, we share social solutions, reminding ourselves how to organise villages in a way that is grounded in traditions, such as the buffalo bank, the rice bank and organic farming practices. Then, of course, we teach meditation — a very crucial aspect. In this part of the world, people are deeply rooted in spiritual practices. But then they are educated in modern schools, and uprooted from their culture. We want to reverse that. We are dreaming of a different kind of education, more holistic, so that the spiritual aspect becomes a natural part of life again. The fifth element is capacity building around management skills — learning how to organise an NGO.

183

Looking back, I must say that we have not been able to change the situation as much as we wanted to. Increasingly, people were confronted with Western advertisements, lured to a more consumerist approach and life has been changing, not always for the better. In the last two years, Jane, colleagues and I have been working with Metta Development Foundation, a National Myanmar NGO with intensive eco-leadership training for middle-management. Metta are now considering how they can adopt ecovillage strategies for sustainable development throughout their programmes.

Ecovillage Transition in Thailand and China

Today we are regularly invited to teach in many regions of Thailand and in Southern China. Yes, many people in China are also longing for a sustainable lifestyle. We are sometimes stopped by the police but, still, it is possible to teach in China.

Our own country, Thailand, is going through deep change. Since 2003, the society is fractious. We are not directly involved in any fighting, but we use the situation to propose changes that go to the root of current issues:

reconnection to nature, spirituality, community building. After the *coup d'etat*, our democracy became slightly stronger, and I have become more involved in the grassroots movement.

One governor from Northern Thailand decided to transition a whole region into an eco-region. 11 villages with 5,000 people were involved. We were asked to redesign the development policy of the whole region. With our experience we were able to bring academia and village people together. We formed a bridge between experts and villagers. Together we created a community master plan and proposed it to the governor. But then he was forced to move, to leave the region and become a governor of another region. And now we have to see whether the next leader of that area will continue the project. The governor had promised us 10 million Baht (approximately 250,000 Euro) as payment for the work done, but then he left and the money could not be transferred. Sadly, corruption is prevalent.

Water and Forest

One of our most important projects is a holistic forest project. Forests are a very critical topic all over South East Asia. Forests are burnt, and as a consequence the water situation becomes a problem. Some districts already have droughts, and the groundwater table is receding so farms and households lose access to water. It requires a new paradigm to consider the renewal of an ecosystem as a whole. Agriculture was sustainable before development came to the region, so now we get rice and vegetable producers together and connect them with traditional and modern knowledge about organic agriculture and water management.

Over the years the community of the Ashram have created a nature paradise on their site.

Economy

The economic system does not support the development of ecovillages. The surplus from every village is sucked out of the region by the banking system. We are thinking about an alternative ethical bank which is based in the region to help us to keep the surplus and the money cycles within the village and region so that local economies can start thriving again.

Last year, we started to connect the ecovillage work with the business world to create a Business of Change. My younger brother started this initiative. His company is one of the top ones in the country. He got sick and had a very deep, life-changing crisis. Since he came back to business, he began opening-up towards spirituality, trying to change the business world from the inside. The main aim of his business has expanded — instead of only maximising profit, its aim is to support the people and the planet.

With ecovillages we don't need to follow the Western development model. We develop in our own way. The most critical message of ecovillages is: we are good enough already. We don't have to catch up with the West. Television and the modern educational system has brainwashed people and told them that they are only good enough if they are Westernised. Yes, we will apply knowledge from the modern world, but this does not mean that we are not good enough. We are good enough, even if we don't aim for a career in the high-rise buildings of Bangkok.

185

Keywords for Solution Library:

Buffalo Bank, Rice Bank — reestablishing traditional economic systems without money
Spiritual Activism — applying spiritual practices and principles to work for social and environmental justice
solution.ecovillage.org

A Gardener in South India

Auroville / India

In South East India, we find one of the world's most highly regarded and largest ecovillages: Auroville. Based on the vision of Sri Aurobindo and Mira Alfassa (known as the 'Mother'), the 'Universal City' was inaugurated in 1968. Today, more than 2,000 people from over 40 countries live permanently in Auroville. For 45 years, Joss Brooks has been working for the ecological restoration of the once-barren plateau and the re-establishment of the indigenous tropical forest. He reflects on his journey, and on how Auroville has shared its experience with the surrounding Tamil communities and thus has learnt from one of the seed cultures of the planet, while sharing innovative ideas from many different societies.

Joss Brooks

Joss Brooks

I grew up in the Island of Tasmania. Until British colonisation in 1804, one of the most ancient aboriginal peoples lived harmoniously in a garden of mountains, grasslands and beaches, which sustained them for over 35,000 years. Their rock art reflected their dreaming. The European invasion destroyed these ancient tribes, and in 1876 the last Tasmanian aboriginal, Queen Truganini, died.

Years later, the first green political party on the planet was formed in Tasmania. People protested against the cutting of old-growth forests and the damming of wild rivers. They were walking in the footsteps of the indigenous peoples who had successfully protected the beauty of nature here for centuries.

After many journeys, I found myself in Tamil Nadu, the garden of the Coromandel Coast in India. Signs of an earlier environmental harmony were still to be found in the sacred groves and temple forests where indigenous plants were protected. I heard about a place near Pondicherry where a vision for a city of the future was being implemented, a vision that had come through Sri Aurobindo and Mira Alfassa. It was to be a place that belonged to nobody in particular, a place for humanity as a whole.

UNESCO and the Indian government supported the idea, and in February 1968, to symbolise the unity of humanity, soil from 120 countries was placed in an urn at the centre of a plateau. When the crowds went home, the site was left to the hot winds from the Bay of Bengal. Seekers, travellers, and wide-eyed refugees from the 1960s' student revolutions became the first pioneers that came to build Auroville.

188

*By planting hundreds of thousands of trees, Joss Brooks and his team
have reforested the area around Auroville
including the Pitchandikulam Forest*

Photo: Joss Brooks

Contact with the Soul of the Forest

The people who were drawn here came from some 30 countries. We built simple huts to live in, our teachers were farmers and illiterate old ladies, who could relate stories for hours and knew hundreds of medicinal plants. In the nearby villages life was hard, yet the age old patterns and ceremonies reminiscent of past, great civilisations of southern India were still in evidence. Even today, temple chariots carrying deities are pulled around the villages at sacred times. The chariots are made of the same wood as the temple door, and oil pressed from seeds of the same tree burns brightly in lamps of the inner sanctum. 500 years ago, poets sang of the animals, birds and plants of this area and their poems were engraved on temple walls. Records exist of a Maharaja being stopped here by a herd of elephants living in dense forests only 200 years ago. So we know of the forest that grew here.

Mirra Alfassa, also called the Mother, who was the driving force behind the manifestation of Auroville, advised us to connect to the spirit of the forest: "it hasn't gone away; a couple of centuries is nothing. This contact to the spirit is even more important than making compost," she said. "The invisible beings will help you to bring back what was there before."

We learnt from the gentle way in which the farmers move water and channel it into the rice fields. They sing while working — you can't sing to a diesel motor. They taught us the rhythms of the year. Ceremonies are still strong in South India. Even bank managers and teachers still go firewalking at the height of summer, calling the rains to come.

We drilled the first wells 150 feet down into the laterite soil. Windmills were erected of wood with cloth sails. We needed shade to survive the long hot summers. We started nurseries, and nurtured the newly planted seedlings with water brought by bullock carts. When the huge monsoon storms came, the fragile plateau eroded badly. We learned about the important watershed concept, we learned that we all live downstream. The sea turned red with the soil as the very foundations of our future township were being washed away. We initiated the healing process: thousands of kilometers of bunds and levees were made across the landscape. Tropical rains need to stay on the land, and soak in to replenish the water table! We made sure dams were built in gullies.

As ground-cover slowly emerged, birds brought seeds and the indigenous flora started to reappear. We mapped the small remnants of original forest in the region, most of it found in the form of temple groves protected by the statues of the local gods and saints. We collected seeds and learnt germination techniques. Through research we understood that the Tropical Dry Evergreen Forest was the most endangered forest type in India. The work in the last decades has been to re-establish 1,000 acres of protected forest as part of the Auroville greenbelt, and to work on projects to bring back this vegetation along the Coromandel Coast. Now Auroville is swathed in a diverse green garment.

Work in the Region

We worked with the people of our watershed to help document their knowledge of the natural resources, particularly tapping into the wisdom of traditional healers. Indigenous knowledge about the animals, vegetables, minerals, traditional technologies and medicinal plants constitutes some of the most precious wealth of a nation. Medicinal forests were established; women's groups made traditional herbal medicines for ethno-veterinary treatment camps, and the cows and goats grew healthier.

Thirty kilometers from Auroville, in order to support local communities, we adopted a government school with 600 children and four teachers, two trees to give shade, and no water and no toilets. We dug a well, built toilets and waste water treatment systems incorporating solar panels and wind mills. The children helped put together teaching materials about their environment. They wove their knowledge into stories, poems, plays and puppet shows and then organised events to share this with the whole village. The school has improved its pass rates from 10% ten years ago to 75-80% today.

But with this comes another problem: now that the children are educated, they are all leaving the village! In rural India, as everywhere else, huge demographic shifts are taking place due to urban migration. The challenge is to bring back new energy and enterprises to the rural sector, so that people don't end up in the slums of Chennai or Pondicherry. Auroville has a number of answers to this, and can be a place that inspires solutions for sustainability, biodiversity and long-term prosperity for the countryside. Recently the Tamilnadu government has proposed the creation of a Sustainable Livelihood Institute on the edge of the township, as a collaborative project based on our holistic approach, with Auroville as its wider campus.

Alternatives for the City

We were given the opportunity to participate in the challenges of urban India. Chennai, 100 km north of Auroville, is a city with 10 million inhabitants. Its officials came to us and said, "Would you be willing to bring the best of Auroville to the middle of Chennai?"

There was a 60 acre wetland full of 50 years of garbage and building rubble and something had to be done about it. We didn't look at this as a 60 acre site, but instead saw it as a watershed of 2 sq. kilometers, and started to involve the people around it. It took a year to make the plan. Eventually we moved 60,000 tons of rubbish to more appropriate places. 200,000 trees of 186 indigenous species were brought from Auroville's nurseries.

Photo: Joss Brooks

Spiritual rituals are still alive and some banyan trees are considered sacred.

We restored the whole complex wetland ecology in the middle of the city. Birds, fish, and crabs returned to the environment. People now enjoy the wetland trails where, before, there had only been wasteland. We made it beautiful, creating spaces with rocks and paintings, environmental information and opportunities for relaxing. And we brought examples of our technologies — flow forms, water treatment systems, vortex fountains, windmills. We wanted to create a place where people could dream again, a place that is wild, where you can heal yourself.

These are all examples of hope. But the reality is as complicated as India is complicated. Auroville essentially means: people from all over the world mixing with these incredible Dravidian people, trying to forge a way forward. What matters most is to see the soul everywhere, in each possible transformation of matter. Within the soul lies the memory of the future garden.

www.auroville.org

191

Keywords for Solution Library:

Ecorestoration — regenerating natural environments
Traditional Knowledge Base — preserving local heritage and wisdom for future generations
solution.ecovillage.org

The Secret of Community

Narara Ecovillage / Australia

After having been deeply involved in the development of Findhorn and the Global Ecovillage Network, John Talbott moved to Australia where he has helped to set up the emerging Narara Ecovillage.

John Talbott

Photo: Richard Cassels

John Talbott

After a three year stint as an English major at university, I changed to engineering, not having any idea what I wanted to do in the world, but pretty sure that I'd at least be able to land some kind of job. I was right about that and spent the first four years after university working for a large multinational, building oil tankers and railroad cars. It was a great experience, learning how big corporations work. But after a couple years I knew I'd need something more meaningful!

It was in 1978 that I came across a place called Findhorn and all kinds of internal bells went off. Before I knew it I had moved around the world and joined this 300-strong spiritual community in the north of Scotland. I'd assumed that I'd abandon engineering and work in the beautiful gardens, blissfully becoming more attuned to nature. That lasted a couple of weeks before I was asked to help in the maintenance department.

During that first year, the early ideas of ecovillages emerged: human settlements reflecting the essential connection to the land, but holding a planetary consciousness/awareness as well. How to express our lofty concepts in built environments? I spent the next twenty-four years developing those ideas and helping to put Findhorn firmly on the ecovillage path. It was an awe-inspiring journey, including helping with the formation of GEN and serving on the GEN board during the first years. It was on a trip to Australia in 1996, during a permaculture event that GEN was participating in, that I met my future wife, an Aussie native.

Building an ecovillage on the ruins of an old farm.

Narara Ecovillage

In late 2003 my wife and I left Findhorn 'for a year', moving to Sydney to be near her family and take a break. As so often happens in life, stuff happens: we've been in Australia ever since. For the last three years I have found myself deeply involved with a new ecovillage, an hour north of Sydney. Narara Ecovillage, founded by Lyndall and Dave Parris, began with a realisation that Lyndall had on her 50th birthday: that most humans function best and are happiest when 'in community' — living together in supportive groups, sharing the ups and downs of life. She soon discovered the ecovillage model was a great fit, incorporating community, but also ecology, economy and worldview in a human scale settlement. On her journey Lyndall put on monthly events, organised outings and generally created interest in the idea of building an ecovillage near Sydney. Soon there was a small following of people keen to help, and their search for the ideal property began, looking at over one hundred properties before finding 'the one' in 2008.

Owned by the state government, the property had been a horticultural research station for more than a hundred years, with many structures already in place. It had been rezoned for 120 suburban lots, standard suburbia. Modern planning practice has evolved into a 'keep everything separated' model, with residential isolated from commercial, where businesses have to be in Business Parks, industries in Industrial Parks and retail shops are in Shopping Centres, and none of them close together. Ecovillages want to mix it all up, just as traditional villages did before the advent of the car, with community's shops, businesses, social activities, residences all close together, within walking distance ideally, and for practical reasons also multi-purpose, multi-use. For example, the village hall hosted meetings one evening and theatre or music events the next; served as a crèche on weekdays, indoor market on weekends; commerce happened around the village square during the day but the same square became the social hub in the evening. People lived above their shops, or had their workshops in outbuildings in the back garden.

Given the fairly fundamental differences between ecovillages and suburbia, it was risky to assume that what the group wanted would be permitted. In the end, the group faced a stark choice: either take the risk with an unconditional offer or let it go. The decision had to be made in less than three weeks.

The first problem was there was no legal entity in place to collect funds from prospective community members to make an offer. The second problem was that no one had asked the interested people on the mailing list (about 600 at the time) whether they would be willing to actually put in money. If they were, how much and under what conditions? Lastly, there was the added twist that Lyndall, the one person that everyone knew, happened to be in a campervan somewhere in the Norwegian fjord country for a couple of months!!

Ecovillage Lesson No. 1

The 'ask' looked impossible in the time frame. But here is Ecovillage Lesson No. 1: when the time is right, miracles happen. And several did happen in those first weeks. Our only legal structure available was a co-operative, a good fit philosophically as well. In a record-breaking time of under two weeks, thanks to a generous lawyer who offered to do the legal work at no upfront cost, The Narara Ecovillage Co-operative was born. First and second miracle, as 'lawyer working for free' should definitely count!

Next, the mailing list was approached to see if the critical mass was there. We needed $5m, with a goal of raising a minimum of 80% in pledges as a measure of enough commitment. Emails were sent out, a meeting called and about forty turned up in person and signed pledges. Over the next ten days more pledges streamed in and on the day of the deadline of August 1st, 2012 the target of A$4m was reached!! Third miracle.

A harrowing month long wait ensued before the offer was formally accepted and suddenly the project was real!

Photo: Richard Cassels

Creating community is the core of every ecovillage development.

195

Called by the Land

I got involved with Narara very much like the way I got involved with Findhorn. While I had met Lyndall and Dave and their team soon after arriving in Australia, I was having a break from 'ecovillages', and starting another project from scratch just wasn't on the cards. But over the years we stayed in touch and I gave a few talks about Findhorn and GEN, and even visited the property a few times once they'd found it.

When the crunch came in early July 2012, with Lyndall overseas there was literally no one who had the time to take on this seemingly impossible task, and it looked as though the window would be missed. On a ferry ride home, watching the sunset over Sydney Harbour I got a clear 'call' from the land. The forested slopes of Narara valley appeared, the open spaces of the floodplain, the views from the hillside, all stunningly beautiful. And I had to ask myself whether what was I doing was more important than supporting the materialisation of such a potentially wonderful project?

The years at Findhorn have been invaluable for me. Findhorn was twenty years old when we started the ecovillage project there in the early 80s; the community's social, cultural and spiritual 'infrastructure' was well established. All I needed to focus on was the ecology and economy. With Narara, not only were we doing the physical master plan, planning and building, we were also needing to establish the community, the unique culture and social coherence that would be the 'glue' of this future village. Now, two and a half years later, with our development applications approved and infrastructure construction soon to commence, the community is 140 strong and thriving. The ecovillage model is working well for Narara.

Mainstream Ecovillage

What is particularly significant about Narara is that it's an ecovillage for the mainstream. This was always an aspiration of GEN's, recognising that the huge task of transforming human settlements around the planet had to apply directly to our Western developed world where the biggest ecological footprints are generated and the biggest transformation needed. Ecovillage solutions need to be transferable to ordinary people to be relevant.

Narara is accessible to a major urban centre and seeking to be an example of integrated mixed-use sustainable development. We've been proactive in engaging our local neighbours and keeping them informed of what we're aiming to achieve, something that we didn't do very well at Findhorn in the early days. Regular communication, open days, public meetings and even grapefruit sharing with the abundance of citrus we had on the land. This had practical benefit as well: we had less than a handful of objections to our development plans because locals were well informed and had been given the opportunity to have their concerns addressed before hearing about them in the paper. Council was able to give their approval much faster.

A spin-off from the local engagement has been our outreach arm, Narara Eco Living Network. Its one-day festival of sustainability called 'Ecoburbia' is an initiative to show people how to create ecovillage living in their own suburb, from renewable energy to building community. One concern we had was being seen to be building a nice cozy green enclave that would be isolated from locals. What we really want to do is promote sustainable living everywhere, seeing Narara Ecovillage as an opportunity to demonstrate this and inspire people to apply the principles in their own homes and neighbourhoods. The festival was opened by the Mayor of Gosford and had two and a half thousand people attend, far more than we expected, but a great indicator that people are really keen to know more.

Ecovillage Lesson No. 2

The time is right and people all over the world are ready and wanting to know solutions.

Our members are really 'pretty normal' for such an out-of-the-box development. But we share the belief that humanity has to change the way we are living on planet Earth. The commitment to make this project happen has been awe-inspiring given the high risk we've had to face. The members are the developers, the funders, the clients and the future residents. Often, they are also providing know-how and physical energy to do the work, be it community-building, or engineering. The collective power of a diverse group coming together to do something significant shouldn't be underestimated.

Ecovillage Lesson No. 3

Resources are often right in front of you: together, we are greater than the sum of ourselves as individuals.

Both our professional advisors and the local council have resonated with the ecovillage vision and have often gone beyond their remit to help us. The NSW planning laws are exceptionally complex and we are 'outside the box' in almost every aspect of the regulations, so this 'extra' help has been essential.

Ecovillage Lesson No. 4

Fortune Favours the Brave — be bold, sound the note, speak the vision and people with the skills needed will appear to help it manifest.

Still a year away from house construction and about a third of the way towards the final target of around 400 residents, we'll probably need a few more miracles before we're done. But more than anything else what has brought us together and helped us survive the first years of our ecovillage creation is the power of community.

No doubt that is what will also carry us forward.

Keywords for Solution Library:
Intergenerational Living — creating spaces for young and old to live together
Bush Care — regenerating native flora and fauna

Solutions for a Vulnerable Climate Zone

Bangladesh

Boniface Subrata, 63, can look back on a life of passionate and patient dedication to community empowerment in his country, Bangladesh. Through sheer tenacity of spirit, he has succeeded in adapting knowledge gained in ecovillages worldwide to local circumstances, in order to reduce poverty and increase local climate change resilience and adaptation. Thus many villages are integrating ecovillage design processes.

Photo: Leila Dregger

Boniface Subrata

Boniface Subrata

Early Beginnings

I was born into the Christian minority of Bangladesh and originally wanted to become a priest. However, during my studies, when I noticed how luxurious the lives of the priests were in comparison with the poverty of so many, I decided to leave. I went to university, and formed a Bangladeshi Christian Students movement. In that time I became known amongst people. They said, "he speaks little, but speaks well". I gained many friends.

After university, I was offered prestigious jobs by international organisations. But, again, I saw the same pattern: the leaders had large houses, while the rest of the people were poor. I called my circles of friends and teachers, ex-priests and ex-nuns together, and said, "Let us do something! In Bangladesh hundreds of thousands are starving!" In July 1991, we formed the Bangladesh Association for Sustainable Development — BASD.

We started to work with some of the poorest communities. Now, looking back after 20 years, these communities have enough to eat and safe homes. What we did was simple: we taught them to save money, even from the little income they had, maybe only 1-2 cents a week. They had never before learnt to make savings. But the small amounts would accumulate and eventually make a crucial change possible. At some point, they would be able to buy a goat or a little piece of land and then they could really improve their lives.

Some of the most sorry plights in Bangladesh are those of the tea workers. They and their families stay on tea plantations. They earn no more than 50 cents/day. They are landless, with no other options. There is no schooling for children, and no access to medicine. Mortality rates are high. Many of them secretly cross the border to India in order to steal some bamboo or fruits, as they don't have enough food. Many are beaten or shot in the process. The situation is humiliating, like modern slavery. The workers cannot protest because there are so many unemployed people waiting to take their places. As they are very religious, we told them, "Will Allah give you food? No, he will tell you to use your brain." Again, we encouraged them to save small amounts from what little income they had.

199

Standing on Our Own Feet

In 1995, a German NGO offered loans to help us build on the vocational training we were offering to villagers. With these loans, we built workshops and equipped them with hand looms made of bamboo. However, three years later, in 1998, there was a serious flood. Waters rose and workshop spaces were flooded for 3 months. All the looms rotted. We were helpless. The business had to be closed down, and people could not pay their loans back. We tried to ask donors for understanding and support, but all funding was frozen.

At that time, 135 people were working with me. I had to tell them: "I am sorry, friends. If you want to stay with me, you are welcome. If you want to try and find better jobs, please go. But I will not stop our work. I will eat only if you can eat. Together, we have to find a different way."

Together, we developed plans that would keep us independent from outside donations in the future. The key point was to re-start BASD and extend our saving programmes. We initiated saving groups in various villages, using small amounts of interest to pay for our staff. We offered vocational training, and equipped workshops for tailoring, batik, electronic repairs, furniture making, etc. Additionally we ran a healthcare program, primary school education, and many kinds of non-formal education for elderly people.

After 10 years of working, by 2012 we were fully self-sufficient. Without any outside funding, we were able to cover the costs of our own work, including administration and staff. At that point, the donors regained interest and started reaching out to us again.

Photo: Boniface Subrata

The first of many EDE courses that — together with permaculture design courses — have changed the lives of many villages in Bangladesh.

Introducing Permaculture and Ecovillage Design

In 1999 I met an Australian permaculture teacher and one of GEN´s founders, Max Lindegger, in India. Later, in 2003, he invited me to be part of a permaculture training in Sri Lanka. In 2005, I participated in Ecovillage Design Education (EDE) in Australia. From then on, my journey was connected to the ecovillage and permaculture networks. Today, I am a leading member of GENOA and on the board of GEN International. Max

Lindegger, May East and Kosha Joubert are my best friends.

Inspired by my experiences in Sri Lanka and Australia, I offered to share my knowledge with my neighbours. But they said, "this has nothing to do with our lives". I was really sad. It was not easy to transmit these new ways of seeing. Max Lindegger advised me to go ahead and try again. I visited tribal villages in the hills, people who were working in tea plantations, very poor but with big hearts. And they accepted me. I worked there for 2 years, supporting them through participatory ecovillage design processes. Unfortunately, in the end, cultural differences emerged. Apparently, I had done too little to really understand their culture and their view of the world. I had to stop working with them.

With all the inner learnings from that experience, in 2007 I started working in a village called Andharmanic. After talking to villagers about permaculture, 14 families joined me to create a permaculture garden, showcasing various kinds of composting and waste management. In parallel, we started a cultural group, sharing traditional songs. A participatory process ensued: every month, more villagers came together to discuss their problems and to plan their future.

Then people from another village in Banishanta, in the delta area of Bangladesh, saw the results from the permaculture garden. They wanted to join. I offered EDE courses for farmers and community leaders from both villages. If you visit these villages today, you will find examples of all four dimensions of ecovillage design: their cooperatives and participatory processes are a rich expression of the social dimension of sustainability; they have thriving local economies; a rich spiritual and cultural programme, celebrating local traditions, and beautiful ecological activities.

In 2008, two more neighbouring villages showed interest. This time it was the farmers of the first villages who talked to them about ecovillages and permaculture, not me.

Then, I met May East, who had worked with GEN and Gaia Education for many years. She saw the good activities going on and put us in contact with the Scottish government. With their assistance, we have now extended our activities to 42 villages in Banishanta, Kulna and Mongla areas of southern Bangladesh, reaching out to more than 30,000 people. These communities are extremely vulnerable to tidal surges and river erosion. All of these villages have now gained access to ecovillage approaches: many inhabitants have participated in permaculture and EDE courses. At least 25 households in each of the villages have started implementing new designs and techniques. These households function as multipliers, so we see the knowledge spreading. We have also trained 326 teachers and members of local authorities, and they start and support small projects: fisheries, organic gardens, nurseries, vermiculture — earth worm composting, etc. The projects are performing really well and improving prosperity in these villages.

The Ecovillage Programme

We adapted the ecovillage programme to fit the specific situation of villages in Bangladesh. Many of our villages are remote; we can only reach them with the help of bikes and boats, and by crossing huge, tidal rivers. Levels of illiteracy and gender inequality are high. Most women work in the home and farm small kitchen gardens. The men farm and fish and sell the products in the markets of nearby towns.

Through BASD, we help to form cooperatives and savings groups in every village. Then, we find out who the 'ecofriendly' people are; those who are ready to become change-makers for sustainability are taught about ecovillage and permaculture design. Women are always on the frontline. In all 42 villages, women are playing much stronger roles now. In the last local elections, several women were elected as local leaders, which had never happened before.

Our staff of volunteers attend the meetings of new groups to support them, but later leave them to continue on their own. When there is a conflict, we are sometimes called in again. However, we encourage the village people to solve their own conflicts. We sit with them, listen, and possibly offer some ideas on conflict resolution. After two years the groups become fully independent.

Boniface Subrata cooperates with politicians and entrepreneurs, and with the Minister of the Environment.

Climate Change Adaptation

Bangladesh is one of the places on Earth most endangered by climate change. Cyclones and floods increasingly hit our country, year after year. All 42 villages are situated close to the ocean. It is very hard to improve life in the villages while they are repeatedly hit. After long discussions, in 2012 we formed the Climate Change Mitigation and Adaptation Network in Bangladesh. We initiated a small-scale relief programme, integrating best practices from the Permaculture and Ecovillage programmes.

We introduced the following climate change adaptation practices in the villages:

- High floors and low ceilings in houses;
- Houses are tied with ropes so that they are not easily blown away;
- Cow stables and toilet floors are raised higher;
- Every village has dry containers in which food, water and documents can be kept;
- More hanging and climbing vegetables;
- Registering centres and management committees help old and vulnerable people find support;
- Advance warning systems in all villages.

360 households so far have started to apply the above, and others are following. Our journey is adventurous and ongoing — the dream of healthy, strong communities and villages in Bangladesh is unfolding one step at a time.

203

Keywords for Solution Library:
Flood Disaster Adaptation Techniques — enhancing chances of survival in some of the most vulnerable communities
Houseroof Gardens — creating areas for protected food cultivation
Tools of Self-reliance and Empowerment - enhancing mutual support in communities
solution.ecovillage.org

Creative Judaism and Ecological Consciousness

Kibbutz Lotan / Israel

Kibbutz Lotan, founded in 1983, in the Southern Arava desert, is one of the last Kibbutzim established in cooperation with the Israeli government and was the first Kibbutz to become a member of the Global Ecovillage Network. With its many ecological activities it is a catalyst for environmental consciousness in Israel — and for liberal Judaism. Alex Cicelsky is a founding member and shares his story.

Alex Cicelsky

Alex Cicelsky

I was 18; my first year of college was in Israel, on a leadership training program in Jerusalem and on a Kibbutz. Even though I couldn't speak the language, I quickly felt at home as people were genuinely helpful and caring. Most people I met were volunteers in organisations concerned with peace and coexistence, social justice and other charity organisations. The Kibbutz was particularly fascinating. It was a place where utopian ideas of society met with the realities of an inclusive modern community.

The Kibbutzim where I volunteered were devoid of religion. Growing up in the USA I learned that being Jewish was both a spiritual experience and a directive toward creating a just society. I found the concept of a secular Jewish Israeli culture both shocking and fascinating.

Kibbutz Lotan was established as a pioneering community experiment, combining the ideals of egalitarian society with creative and liberal Jewish expression, and a political agenda of disengaging religion from government. We were a group of 60 young adults, aged 18 to 24, from both Israel and other countries around the world. Lotan is located in the Arava desert, a sparsely populated region with no territorial conflicts. It is one of the last Kibbutzim to be established as part of a government policy of setting up intentional agrarian communities. At the age of 21, after studying agriculture in the US, I moved to Israel and became a founding member of Kibbutz Lotan.

Alex Cicelsky

Building a Geodeisic Dome in the EcoCampus.

Economic Development

A Kibbutz is a legally recognised and supervised cooperative entity. The government assisted us with housing. Our income was based on the winter export of melons, tomatoes, onions and corn, all of which were grown in sand with brackish water. Agricultural and management advisers from older Kibbutzim tutored us. I picked vegetables, sorted dates, fixed tractors and dreamed of building a dairy farm. A few years later we were given a milk production quota and loans to build a dairy farm which now produces over 3 million litres of milk a year and supplies us with a constant income

205

that seasonal vegetables never could. Today, our dates are considered the best in the country — and are irrigated with treated waste water from Eilat.

These 'milk and honey' branches are the backbone of our economy. However, our economy has always left us struggling to survive. For thirty two years we were an income sharing commune, supplying all of the needs of our members. Housing, food, healthcare, transportation, electricity, water, education and access to education and cultural activities were available to families, based on the number and age of children and in consideration of special needs. We tried numerous initiatives to increase our income, including a goat dairy, cheese making and manufacturing machines to process vegetables, but none of these was profitable. We acquired debt to develop agriculture and maintain the community — and the repayment has been a constant burden and a deterrent to attracting new members.

The Upbringing of Children

Communities are living, changing organisms that need to respond creatively to internal and external forces. Big changes came about when the first members of the Kibbutz became parents. Although historically some Kibbutzim raised children separately from the parents because of health issues (malaria infested swamps) and later because of educational philosophies, we chose to live in nuclear families as do all Kibbutzim now. Tensions around scheduling work and financing childcare are discussed in long community meetings. There has always been a tradition of 'openly speaking one's thoughts and emotions', which is both provocative and essential.

Financial security has been a constant struggle. Kibbutzim in our region agreed to pay off our high interest loans from banks. In return we repay them at low interest rates. Funding the 'luxurious simplicity' of rural, communal living in our region is a challenge because of the high cost of electricity and well water. In our desert climate, there's almost no rain which means all water must be purchased!

60 of the 280 Kibbutzim in Israel are still income-sharing communes. The rest allow for differential pay, income independence and private ownership of houses. We changed this year from income-sharing to private ownership and income to stimulate entrepreneurship. This also makes us more attractive to young couples interested in joining and building their homes in our community. Our Kibbutz budget pays for community services, youth education, a supplemental health fund, supplemental pension payments for members with low wages, and cultural events. Members can work for the Kibbutz, but the number of jobs is limited. Many of us work as teachers and social workers in our region.

Ecological Education

In 1996 we developed our educational branch: The Center for Creative Ecology (CfCE) and joined GEN-Europe in 2001. We were involved with the development of Gaia Ecovillage Design Education and the spread of permaculture in Israel. We spearheaded community recycling, construction from waste materials, straw-bale and natural construction, urban gardening and composting. Our Bird and Nature Reserve, built in an abandoned sand quarry, is a model for protecting the millions of birds that migrate between Europe and Africa. Our Tea House was the first solar restaurant in Israel. Our organic gardens are a training centre for teachers and activists who have gone on to establish other education centres and urban gardens in Israel and around the world.

We've made some important discoveries. Advisers and farmers taught us that only a limited number of vegetables could be grown in our region using industrial fertilisers and regimens of pesticides and herbicides. We succeeded in eliminating all these chemicals by using compost and companion planting. The large variety of plants is an oasis, and is considered by international birders to be one of Israel's top 'hot spots'. We debated whether we should focus on ecological training or large scale organic farming and decided to focus on education!

My academic interest evolved from agriculture to architecture. I've become a researcher and planner of energy efficient buildings. We passed the fire codes, so that earth-plastered straw-bale houses can now be built legally. We've built houses that use 70% less energy for heating and cooling compared to conventional buildings — a considerable feat in summers when temperatures peak at 40° C daily!

With all our environmental efforts — protection of land — support of bird watching — waste separation — recycling and composting — using renewable energy — energy conserving construction — we have made a direct impact in our region. The region prides itself today on its achievements in renewable energy. Over 50% of the electricity that Eilat uses is produced by solar panels and our region practises significantly more waste separation and recycling compared to other regions. We're proud to be reminded that we were the catalyst for these developments.

The compact photovoltaic system that powers the EcoCampus, where our students live in ten highly efficient passive solar straw-bale houses, produces 5 times more electricity than it needs, even when air conditioners are turned on all summer long. The EcoCampus kitchen uses biogas. We have no-water toilets and a grey-water system to showcase for the 10,000 people who come every year to visit and be inspired by our ecological systems.

The EcoCampus at night.

Alex Cicelsky

Decision Making

Making community decisions, and airing issues publicly is both the challenge and strength of intentional communities. In the beginning everything was discussed in our general assembly. Now more is processed in committees and then resolutions are brought forth for approval. I remember the challenges we faced in the early 80s about accepting gay couples in the community. We were really ahead of the times in Israel. Some members felt threatened and we spent an intensive month processing this issue. A gay couple wanted to join us and they had said that they could only come if they could be openly gay. It turned out to be a beautiful process, everyone learnt a lot, and ultimately people were looking at their own prejudices and were able to say that they wanted to live in a community that supports everyone openly. The process radiated to all the communities in our region. A decade later one of our Kibbutz youth came out as gay and was accepted without ridicule by his peers at home and at school.

Lotan today has around 150 residents. We have 50 adult members and candidates for membership, 70 children and a few grandparents who have retired with us. We have run leadership training for 18-year old Israelis for two decades, focusing on youth education and communal living. We have a 20-room guesthouse and a Watsu (shiatsu in water) spa. Permaculture and Ecovillage Education programme participants live with us constantly.

Guests and our students have initiated spectacular projects around the globe that they say were inspired by what they learned while living with us. Our interpretation of the story of Genesis is that humans were placed in the Garden of Eden to be stewards of nature while developing human habits with care and tolerance. Our vision is to meet that challenge in our community and to teach others to do the same in theirs.

www.kibbutazlotan.org

Keywords for Solution Library:

Saltwater Farming — farming with brackish water in hot/arid environments
Strawbale Building 2 — using strawbales as perfect combination of natural bricks and insulation
Compost Toilets 2 — reducing the use of water while creating natural manure for reforestation
solution.ecovillage.org

209

Overcoming Occupation

Hakoritna Farm / Palestine

The Palestinian farmer, Fayez Taneeb, became a political activist when most of his farm was destroyed by Israeli soldiers — enclosed by the Separation Wall on one side, and a chemical factory on the other. Today he is a farmer again. Together with his wife Muna, he is transforming what is left of their farm into a demonstration and training site for sustainability — a mini-ecovillage.

Fayez Taneeb and Aida Shibli

Aida Shibli, a Palestinian peace activist raised in Israel, a member of the Global Campus and board member of GEN-International, has organised workshops about sustainable technologies for students of agriculture. Together, Fayez and Aida gathered students from universities in the West Bank, experts from within Palestine and abroad, and built exemplary infrastructure for solar energy, biogas, compost toilets and permaculture. More importantly, they are weaving a net of hope in the West Bank, creating a base of knowledge and confidence for the time after occupation.

Aida Shibli, Israeli-Palestinian activist.

Aida Shibli

Even as a child, I could not accept people saying: "things are as they are". I was convinced that things could be changed. During the first Intifada, when I was 16, I created a banner for our balcony with the words: 'Territories for Peace'. One hour later, 16 policemen came to our house. They took me in for one night of investigation.

This experience changed my life. I started to educate myself and discovered all the things that my people did not speak about: the massacres, the displacements. I became a peace activist, working with both Palestinians and Israelis. In 2000, during the second Intifada, I was a nurse and was treating both Israeli soldiers and Palestinian suicide bombers. I understood that it was not about taking sides. It was the system itself that was wrong.

In the middle of an exploding Jerusalem, I found myself pregnant and alone — my husband abandoned me after five months of marriage. I understood that my work should not only be about political peace, but also about peace between man and woman. I made a vow to my unborn child: 'Another life must be possible, and I will search for it.' The vision that I carry is of a planet Earth in abundance. I work wholeheartedly for a free Palestine, but my vision and my inner source go beyond this.

For 10 years I have been holding the vision of a Peace Research Village in the Middle East, where Palestinians, Israelis and Internationals work in mutual support and reconciliation. We have made a lot of effort to achieve this vision. I wanted to expose more fellow Palestinians to this vision. However, whenever we tried to work determinedly in mixed groups of Palestinians and Israelis, we found ourselves being drawn into conflicts about responsibility and the radicalism of injustices. We are not yet able to solve this at the root.

Our conclusion was that, for the coming years, we would separate our work. The Israeli group works in Israeli society, and the Palestinian group focuses on Palestine. I started to create spaces in the West Bank where local communities could meet local experts, protected by international witnesses. With the support of the Global Campus founded in Tamera, Portugal, and the company Lush from the UK, I started this work on the Hakoritna farm in Tulkarem in 2013.

Fayez is a political activist and leader who has become a farmer again. Keeping his farm is his form of resistance.

211

*Even Israeli soldiers become curious what the new project is about —
and are treated in a friendly way.*

212

Sustainability and Autonomy

Creating models for sustainability and autonomy does not just express my
love for the Earth; it is a tool of resistance. I believe that our first freedom
is to liberate ourselves from foreign supply systems for food, energy or
water. Blaming the forces of occupation won't change anything, but using
our knowledge to turn our villages and homes into sustainable models
will be our path towards liberation. Our workshops are not so much about
teaching, but about remembering and sharing the knowledge that is already
there.

One example is the solar dryer. The Palestinian farmers cannot export
their products because of the checkpoints and the wall. They can only sell
inside Palestine, and as products in such a small country are ripe at the
same time, the market is at times flooded with cheap tomatoes, cucumbers
or mandarins. Thus, farmers cannot ask a price that pays for their work,
especially when they grow organic fruits. By establishing the solar dryers,
we created the possibility of preserving fruits and vegetables for the winter,
thus strengthening food sovereignty. When we presented this technology
people said: "We used to dry our products on the rooftops, but we had
to take them down in the evening and put them back up in the morning,
and sometimes it rained and then all was ruined." The solar dryer makes

things easy: a plastic sheet tunnel and solar driven fans to take care of the right humidity. The fruits are dried in one day. Another example: flush toilets were not in our culture originally, but now they consume a lot of our precious water resources. We installed compost toilets to demonstrate an alternative technique — using the fence protecting the separation wall as part of the construction.

For some of the young people, the workshops are the first time they have spent a night away from their parents' home, and to share openly with others. We run women's empowerment groups and talk together about all topics of life: 'What will come after occupation?' is a question that we address, too. Israeli soldiers can become curious and drop by with their guns. Previously, without internationals present, these visits often became nasty. Now, at times they are received with open hands full of fresh strawberries, instead.

The work on the farm is only the beginning. Palestinians today are occupied by the needs of daily living. Travelling from one part of the country to the other is expensive. We are not connected to each other as we used to be. And because there are very few jobs inside Palestine, every morning, thousands of people stand in the line to cross the border with the hope of working some hours in Israel for a tiny salary. Instead of wasting our time at checkpoints and borders, we could do precious work in our country — if we only had models to show us the way.

We know many people who are active in their villages. We visit them. We organise meetings and invite them to connect with each other. We run educational programmes to share our knowledge about solutions and our inner experiences. Meanwhile, all across the West Bank, people know us from the TV and newspapers. What we do is appreciated by the communities. Some of us have the privilege of seeing the wall from both sides. It is our task to share information about the reality on the other side. We will continue transforming pain into hope, no matter how extreme and challenging the situation is. We want to see Palestine green and free.

Fayez Taneeb

The Israeli authorities confiscated 80% of our farm to build the wall and chemical factories; now there only 2 hectares left. We have tried to fight the destruction nonviolently, without success. However, the core of the farm has endured in the middle of all this damage. For me, this is a miracle. This was my motivation to start this project and create a place for hope. Since we started, numerous university students, journalists, women's organisations, and supporters from outside Palestine and from the local communities, have come to witness this model of resistance and are inspired.

213

Fayez Taneeb, owner of Hakoritna Farm.

Tulkarem is a special place because of the forest that spreads throughout the city, along the streets and everywhere. We plant many trees! Tulkarem's people are known for their generosity and openness, hosting visitors with a warm heart. We also have famous local products such as the sweetest ice cream in the world! Every morning, Muna and I walk 10 kilometers to the farm by foot, and we stay there most of the day. On the farm I feel the deep connection with the earth, the sense of belonging to it, and the connection to Nature and our products.

We have workers and women working with us. For the new ecological and environmental achievements of the farm and the entire alternative infrastructure, it is either Muna, or our son Oday, or me who supervises and takes care of it. Oday has acquired a wide knowledge and might be the next one to take the flame and hold the vision. Every day we work with the solar dryer. In each season we have different fruits to experiment with. Last year, we dried loquats, citrus fruits and grapes. Beyond that, we have established permaculture methods on the farm: we have a seed bank, a biogas system and compost toilets.

It has always been our way of life to be generous, to give something to people we meet, and to help people in different aspects of their life. We aim to keep the spirit of collaboration with each breath. Carrying a noble message to others is what makes us human beings. Our message now is about clean food and clean living — that is, food that doesn't contain pesticides and a way of living that does not destroy the natural systems around us, but helps to regenerate them.

*The Farm is clamped between the Separation Wall
and chemical factories.*

215

Struggles and Hope

The occupation in our country is present in every moment of our lives, whether it affects us on an individual level or as a whole community. There are severe environmental problems connected to the occupation: industrial waste is being dumped in our territories, numerous new Israeli settlements located on hill tops release their sewage water to villages and farms down the hill. The 11 chemical factories around Tulkarem were forbidden to operate in Israel because they were categorised as environmentally destructive. Now they have established them here and, as a result, we have the highest rate of cancer in the whole country.

Also, the economy is a challenge: all tools and equipment we need have to be obtained from the system of occupation, which means they are expensive — but our products can only be sold in our local markets for very low prices. We constantly feel the presence of the occupation and work to end it. In the Middle East, we tend to take to violence as a way to deal with injustice. However, I will continue to believe in nonviolence and carry this message with me. What gives me hope is that our young people are starting to hold the vision with us. I can see my future in them. What gives me the strength to continue the work is having an amazing wife like Muna. She has an amazing and generous spirit of giving, creating, holding and persisting: she is unimaginable! Whenever she sees that my energy is going down, and that I am losing hope, she reminds me, and charges me with more faith so that I can carry on.

In my view, humanity is living on one ship, and nobody has the right to damage the spot he is standing on because this will eventually kill us all. The new approaches we share on the farm are like a lighthouse for all the people visiting us. My promise is that I will keep working for a better world and continue the simple but powerful message of producing clean food. I will make the farm a model for many other projects in the West Bank, and trust that in time we will see hundreds of similar projects spreading throughout Palestine. I hope that the Global Campus and GEN-Palestine become a big movement connecting many people all over the country and beyond.

Keywords for Solution Library:

Biogas — using organic waste as energy resource
Solar Dryer — preserving fruits and vegetables in sustainable ways
solution.ecovillage.org

THE HISTORY OF GEN

Global Ecovillage Network: 1991-2015

Ross and Hildur Jackson

Ross and Hildur Jackson, from Denmark, are the 'parents' of the Global Ecovillage Network. Here they share how it started and how they see it developing today.

Introduction

The Global Ecovillage Network (GEN) has existed for 20 years and Gaia Education, which began as a GEN project, is celebrating its 10th year of teaching the principles of living sustainably.

Ecovillages provide models for lifestyles that reduce our ecological footprint while delivering a better quality of life — lifestyles that are possible in all countries of the world. The models are based on solidarity and cooperation and may provide a prototype that can lead to global justice. In ecovillages we are learning how to solve conflicts, how to develop a global consciousness, how to create places where children can grow up in sane and healthy environments, how to use renewable, integrated energy systems, how to provide 100% organic food and how to live lives full of love and compassion.

The ecovillage movement can be seen as a deliberate strategic response to the destructive consequences of the dominant world view. The 'market society' simply doesn't work for the vast majority of people; it can never lead to anything but a degraded environment and a disastrous and widening gap between the rich and the poor.

The ecovillage movement is part of a much larger movement of civil society initiatives that are responding to these issues. When Ken Wilber recommends 'integral practice', he is describing ecovillage living. The 'voluntary simplicity' that Duane Elgin calls for, and the 'sustainable abundance' that Bernard Lietaer describes, can be found in the lifestyles of ecovillagers. When Paul Ray and Ruth Sherry Anderson define the rise of the 'Cultural Creatives', they are describing the values already adopted and implemented by ecovillagers. When Thomas Berry calls for a 'new story of the universe', ecovillagers are already practising this story on the ground. While many other parts of the greater movement focus on important single issues, like climate agreements, renewable energy, economic reforms, etc., ecovillagers play the role of living holistic solutions and 'walking their talk'.

The ecovillage movement's time may have finally arrived. It has laid a firm foundation for people who are aware that we must quickly move to a sustainable and equitable global society, based not on the needs of multinational corporations but on the needs of ordinary people everywhere. We can change society from the bottom up and we are doing it. However, we cannot do it alone. We also need radically revised global trade agreements, a consensus on how to tackle climate change, and real empowerment for people in the poorest countries.

The Origin

The impulse for the Global Ecovillage Network came from an initiative taken by Gaia Trust in 1990. The following article is a personal account of some of the major milestones along the way as seen from our particular vantage point. We have broken it into two parts — 1991-2003 and 2003-2015.

Hildur's story

When Hildur gained her degree as a lawyer in January of 1967, she went to a kibbutz in Israel to explore whether humans were essentially egoistic or not. This had been a recurring discussion with her partner, Ross Jackson. From her time there, she developed a deep conviction that human nature can change and that it's possible to build a better society. She married Ross and had her first baby in February 1968 (the same week that Auroville was founded and student rebellions swept Europe). She began her study of cultural sociology in Denmark to acquire knowledge about bringing about change. For the next 10 years she questioned traditional science, joined and created social movements and co-founded one of the first Danish co-housing projects. Everything seemed possible.

She then heard about a Norwegian Project, The Nordic Alternative Future Project initiated by Norwegian Erik Dammann (founder of The Future in our Hands). The project linked 100 Nordic grassroots movements to the best of the scientific community, in order to create a vision of how to solve global, social and environmental problems. Research councils were created in the different Nordic countries — Hildur worked in the Danish group for ten years as a coordinator and later brought a report, 'Future Letters from the North' to the women's UN meeting in Nairobi. Here she made friends with Wangari Maathai.

What became clear to Hildur was that we have all the knowledge and tools we need to change the world. But we in the North have to put our own house in order, build sustainable communities and give up exploiting the rest of the world. This was her background for co-founding Gaia Trust—a Danish charitable association — in 1987 and for formulating the Gaia Trust's *yin/yang* strategy.

For many centuries, technology and economics (*yang*) have determined how society is organised. Now, it seems the right time for people to decide how they want to live together. Do men and women want to live in harmony with nature in a sustainable and spiritually-satisfying way that is also globally just? This is the *yin* part of the strategy. The *yang* part is to develop technologies that are supportive of this vision.

Ross's Story

Ross's background was quite different, being a management consultant in the private sector specialising in Operations Research with broad experience in many industries. He had for some years been concerned with the neglect of the environment and global trends that tended to increase the gap between rich and poor. He agreed with the conclusions of the Limits to Growth model, that civilisation would be facing formidable problems in the foreseeable future. He was also in agreement with Hildur, that action was most unlikely to come from politicians, who were actually part of the problem.

Ross was attracted to the idea of supporting a network of ecovillages because he saw its strategic potential as a countervailing power to the coming global economic crisis. He believes that as we reach the limits to growth, and if the global economy collapses or it becomes difficult to make a planned transition to a sustainable future, it will be necessary to build a new culture. The foundation of this culture must necessarily be sustainable human settlements, and for these we need good models. Thus a network of ecovillages that provided such models would be an invaluable base on which to build.

219

The Early Years: 1991-2004

Fjordvang 1991

In 1990, Hildur and Ross bought Fjordvang, the former World University, in Western Denmark, which had been an international learning centre for 25 years under the leadership of Aage Rosendal Nielsen. In 1991, Robert and Diane Gilman, editors of *In Context* magazine, moved there with them to build an ecovillage and work on their common cause. As a first step, Gaia Trust commissioned Robert and Diane to survey the field and identify the best examples of ecovillages from around the world. The Gilmans' report to Gaia Trust showed that, although many exciting and vastly different communities existed, a full-scale, ideal ecovillage did not exist. But, together, the existing projects made up a vision of a different culture and lifestyle that had great potential.

Based on the Gilmans' report, twenty people from some of the communities and a few broad thinkers were invited in to discuss how Gaia Trust could best use its funds. The participants included a number of people who would later be key leaders of GEN — Max Lindegger, Declan Kennedy, and Albert Bates—as well as intellectuals outside of the ecovillage sphere, such as Karl-Henrik Robert, founder of The Natural Step, David Korten (who later wrote *When Corporations Rule the World*) and Marilyn Mehlmann of The Global Action Plan. The consensus that the group reached was that Gaia Trust should support the people who were actually living the new paradigm— the ecovillagers — because they were essential for the transition and were receiving no support from elsewhere. It became clear to all that the world needed good examples of what it means to live in harmony with nature in a sustainable and spiritually-satisfying way, in a technologically advanced society.

Which were the first 'ecovillages'? It is a difficult question because many of the communities were founded before GEN existed. In the 1960s, several spiritually-based projects were initiated in different parts of the world: Findhorn in Scotland, The Farm in Tennessee, USA, Sarvodaya in Sri Lanka and the NAAM movement in Burkino Faso. Solheimer in Iceland has roots going all the way back to 1930. The Indian philosopher and sage Sri Aurobindo and his French counterpart, The Mother, put forth the vision of Auroville in India in 1968. So there is no easy answer. As Geoph Kozeny states in his video, Visions of Utopia, the idea of 'community' goes back a long way. Community has been the essence of human culture from time immemorial. But by adopting a new name, the basic concept was infused with new energy.

In 1993, Gaia Trust brought together a number of established and embryonic Danish ecovillages under the Danish Ecovillage Network — the first national network. A second global strategy meeting was called at Fjordvang, with a smaller group focusing strictly on the ecovillage strategy, and a loose network was informally initiated with a secretariat in Denmark funded by Gaia Trust under the daily leadership of Hamish Stewart.

Findhorn 1995

The movement took a major step in 1995. A conference at Findhorn: 'Ecovillages and Sustainable Communities for the 21st Century' was organised by the Findhorn community (led by John Talbot and Diane Gilman) and the evolving informal ecovillage network. It was a great success. The proceedings were published in 1996 by Findhorn Press — *Ecovillages and Sustainable Communities; Models for 21st Century Living*. The conference was attended by over 400 people from forty countries, while another 300 who wished to be there had to be turned away. It was clear that the ecovillage concept had hit a sensitive nerve with a lot of people.

Immediately following this meeting, 20 people from different ecovillages met for five days and the Global Ecovillage Network was formally established. It consisted of three regional networks to cover the globe geographically, with centres at The Farm (USA), Lebensgarten (Germany) and Crystal Waters (Australia) and an international coordinating office at

Gaia Trust, Denmark. Gaia Trust committed to covering the expenses of the network for 3-5 years. The plan was first to focus on forming regional networks that would link existing projects. A second, longer-term goal was set to create global services, like an education network, that would cut across regions, as soon as budgets and manpower permitted.

The founding group at Findhorn

221

UN Habitat II: Istanbul

At the Findhorn meeting it was decided — inspired by Rashmi Mayur's passionate presence — that the movement should join the United Nations Habitat II conference in Istanbul, the following summer. A major exhibition at the NGO forum was built: a long straw bale wall, plastered with clay, became an ideal place for posters with photos from ecovillages around the world. A model windmill, solar cells and running water contributed to a pleasant atmosphere. Hildur had prepared 5,000 copies of a booklet called *The Earth is Our Habitat*, and more than 40 workshops covering all issues of ecovillages and global politics were held. Outside, GEN was in charge of building an old Harran stone house with master builders from the region.

Indian architect Suhasini from Auroville built an attractive and earthquake-resistant house in just five days from mud bricks produced on site with a manual earth-pressing machine.

Hanne Strong instigated our first contact with Ari Ariyaratne from Sarvodaya in Sri Lanka. She had invited 40 spiritual leaders, who in their concluding statement praised ecovillages as an important new concept. Many guests from the official conference visited and praised the GEN exhibition and GEN was invited to address the official UN delegates, with Ross writing and Helena Norberg-Hodge delivering a well-received talk. Istanbul put GEN firmly on the global map.

At the exhibition of the UN Habitat in Istanbul, GEN's straw bale wall with posters from different ecovillages attracted a lot of attention.

Regional Networks

During the next three years networks were built under the leadership of the three regional secretaries, namely Declan Kennedy, Albert Bates and Max Lindegger, the initial GEN board, with coordination by Hamish Stewart, the International Secretary, based at Fjordvang.

This period resulted in the establishment and growth of three autonomous networks covering the globe: The Ecovillage Network of the Americas (ENA), GEN-Europe, which also covered Africa at that time, and GEN Asia/Oceania (GENOA). The GEN board met in many parts of the world during this time.

Gaia Trust Gears Down

In June 2001, Gaia Trust warned that its financial support to GEN would gradually decrease over the next two years. GEN would have to find new sources of funding. This was because it was always Gaia Trust's policy to use its capital over a relatively short period while its founders were still active, and it wanted to ensure that GEN did not become dependent.

223

The GEN Ambassador - Rashmi Mayur

No history of GEN would be complete without mentioning the special role played by the late Dr. Rashmi Mayur, leader of the International Institute for Sustainable Future in Mumbai, India.

Rashmi was unofficially GEN's 'ambassador to the UN'. He participated in all the big conferences as well as many planning meetings. He was an adviser to the UN and several Southern governments.

At the Johannesburg UN Earth Summit of August 2002, Rashmi was appointed official spokesman for the South, and had planned 28 major speeches and workshops. But, tragically, he suffered a debilitating stroke during his first speech, was unconscious for four months, slowly recovered all faculties but passed away in early 2004. He is greatly missed by all his colleagues who carry on his vision to create a more sustainable, more just world.

Spirituality in Ecovillages

It has been exciting to follow and visit so many communities with different spiritual practices. One thing stands out: in a world torn by religious strife, GEN has never had any problems. Quite the opposite, in fact. We have prayed and meditated in all existing traditions and felt enriched and accepted by all. In our international community, people from so many spiritual backgrounds cooperate, accept and love each other. We all have the same values, independent of religion and culture. The world needs this kind of interfaith work.

2004-2015

As forewarned, Gaia Trust was forced to cut back on its level of funding for GEN by a factor of ten after July 2003. For all intents and purposes, GEN became a volunteer organisation.

Education for Sustainability

The idea of creating an educational programme was on the table from the very beginning. By the late 1990s, most of the larger ecovillages were teaching in their regions as they naturally wanted to share their knowledge. They were typically teaching permaculture and sustainability and the design of ecovillages. Some of the larger ones began to call themselves 'Living and Learning' centres, a concept first conceived by Philip Snyder. But there was no universal curriculum.

In 1998, Hildur invited 55 educators from within the ecovillage network to come to Fjordvang, to celebrate Ross's 60th and Max Lindegger's 50th birthdays and to brainstorm around the idea of creating a comprehensive educational programme for sustainability design. This would integrate the concepts of organic farming, permaculture, renewable energy, wastewater treatment, facilitation of meetings, ecological building, conflict resolution, green businesses and economy and much more, into a programme that can be taught at ecovillages and illustrated with on-site field work, based on the 'Living and Learning' concept as a new paradigm in education, i.e. you can live the new lifestyle, while you are learning how to establish and design it.

Hildur took the initiative for a further meeting at Findhorn in June 2004 with 30 invited educators. The starting point was the 'sustainability wheel' described in Hildur and Karen Svensson's book, *Ecovillage Living: Restoring the Earth and Her People*, which was published in 2002.

Gaia Education (see www.gaiaeducation.net) was formally launched in October 2005 at the GEN+10 Conference in Findhorn, and flourished under the wonderful leadership of May East. Since then, GEN and Gaia

Education have worked very closely together, but as two separate entities. The first 'product' was a four week course called Ecovillage Design Education (EDE), which continues to be taught all over the world (in 35 countries at the last count). In 2008 an on-line version of the EDE was developed with the Open University of Catalonia in Barcelona and is scheduled to become an accredited 2-year Master's degree course in its 8th season, 2015/16. The curriculum is now available on the Gaia Education website in 10 languages.

Board Meeting in Huehuecoyotl

After the cutback in 2003, GEN continued to develop over the next six years or so. These were difficult years. A positive aspect was the annual GEN-Europe assembly, which attracted more and more people each year as the ecovillage idea gradually spread, not least to Eastern Europe and Russia. With the introduction of the Gaia Education programme in 2005, new life emerged in many ecovillages — education was seen not only as a vehicle for local outreach but also for generating some income. The free material and a polished curriculum with UNITAR, and UNESCO's stamp of approval made it easy to get started and attract people. Education was becoming an essential part of every ecovillage's story.

Reviving GEN

A new activist phase in GEN's history began with the election of Kosha Joubert as president in 2008. Kosha was one of the 30 educators who had developed the Gaia Education curriculum and she had been very successful in introducing it to her ecovillage, Sieben Linden in Germany, inviting many foreign participants and getting financial support from the German government. One of the major goals of this time was to support the emergence of an independent African network. This was initiated in 2012, with financial help, once again, from the German foreign ministry, and the developments were followed with great interest.

May East, Gaia Education Chief International
Officer, and Kosha Joubert .

A new generation of GEN was very creative in extending its range of activities, and at the same time inspiring increasing momentum in all regions; a more streamlined organisation and broader vision was established; in 2013, an independent South American network — CASA — evolved out of ENA; the youth organisation, NextGEN, flourished.

In December 2012 the world was celebrating the end of one Mayan age and the beginning of a new one. Gaia Trust decided to give 5 rewards to 5 of the initiators and mainstays of GEN and Gaia Education. These were given to Max Lindegger, Albert Bates and Declan Kennedy for building the GEN networks and to May East and Kosha Joubert for being inspiring leaders of Gaia Education and GEN in recent years.

By visiting an ecovillage like Findhorn, Sieben Linden, Tamera, Damanhur, Auroville or Ecovillage at Ithaca, you can experience a new culture emerging. They are all a little different but have in common a holistic culture where people are in a process of change, where the goal is to live a full and joyful social life, while keeping the ecological footprint low, and not forgetting the old GEN saying: "If it ain't fun, it ain't sustainable!"

227

Appendix

How to get involved

If this book inspires you to want to get more involved, you are welcome to join us!

Locally

Find your local ecovillage and offer to volunteer there. It's a good way to get to know the community and see if it is for you. If there are no ecovillages nearby, start asking questions openly why not. You may just find many other people thinking like you.

Nationally

Some countries have national networks of ecovillages that can help you find the ecovillage you are looking for or give you advice on how to start an ecovillage in your country.

If there are ecovillages, you could help network them and maybe work toward a national network. If there are no ecovillages nationally consider becoming a GEN Ambassador, presenting the concept of ecovillages in your area. See our webpages for more details.

Regionally

If you are part of an ecovillage project, consider applying for GEN membership as a full, aspiring or supportive member. GEN is present all over the world and there may be possibilities to volunteer or do an internship at one of their regional offices.

In most cases you must be able to cover your own costs of a room and board. Check if there are grants or scholarships available to support your work. You can also become an online volunteer. It is a great way to gain an overview of what is happening in your region.

Contact us if you are interested in writing your thesis on a sustainable communities-related theme.

Globally

GEN is a global organisation and we want to develop our network where you are. Perhaps you can offer your talents in sustainability, translation, IT, communications and publicity, policy-influencing and fundraising to international working groups that work online. The GEN International office is always interested in receiving volunteers and interns. Unfortunately at the moment we do not have the funds to pay for these interns, so most of our volunteers find their own funding. We like to have interns for at least 3 months.

Wherever you live you can become a Friend of GEN by joining our Friends of GEN campaign, which supports people everywhere trying to make the change that is so necessary. Find more information on our websites!

Interested?

If you feel inspired, why not send us your CV and a motivation letter stating the kind of tasks you would hope to do and what you think you could offer? Please contact us at:

info@ecovillage.org (International)

info@gen-europe.org (Europe)

contact@ecovillage.org (North America)

info@ecovillage.org (CASA)

contact@gen-africa.org (Africa)

welcome@ecovillage.org (Oceania and Asia)

GEN Newsletter

The GEN Newsletter is the main medium of communication of the international ecovillage movement. It is sent out four times a year to over 15,000 addresses worldwide, as well as to policy makers, social media, magazines and newspapers. It is enlivened by contributions from all continents: members of GEN, regional networks, ambassadors, and activists of related movements.

The newsletter is a forum for events, innovations and developments from the world of the ecovillages. On our website gen.ecovillage.org you can download a pdf version or subscribe to it for free.

We look forward to your contribution! Send it to: news@ecovillage.org

NextGEN – GEN´s Youth Organisation

Since 2005, a group of empowered young people have been creating an inspiring movement within the existing ecovillage network. NextGEN is the name of this youth-focused and youth-directed Thematic Network of the Global Ecovillage Network. NextGEN is now building youth-based projects in every region of GEN, and its members represent a wide diversity of young people from around the world.

In 2012 NextGEN experienced a revival and has since been running youth programmes emerging from young people's passionate desire to lead a purposeful life. Their curiosity is the natural foundation of true innovation. Their projects focus on ecological initiatives like permaculture or ecological clubs, on leadership-training, such as learning Sociocracy and Dragon Dreaming — and on international youth exchange between the Global South and Global North, to learn to respect and understand each other. We explore culture, education, art and communication in such a way that previously-unimagined potentials can unfold. The energy generated through group building activities and visioning a future we want, helps to heal old wounds and find new pathways. NextGEN has already proved, in its brief history, that empowering youth is an important step for humanity to be able to withdraw from the current destructive system into a new world. All are invited to join us.

In July 2013, during the annual GEN Conference in Schweibenalp, Switzerland, NextGEN was deeply honoured to receive the Gaia Excellence Award for the most inspiring project of the year. This achievement was primarily due to inspiring presentations from youth-based projects around the world. The award, granted by the General Assembly of Ecovillages, showed a sign of faith and support from the entire GEN community, and redoubled NextGEN's commitment to create a strong youth movement, while keeping the clear connection to GEN.

nextgen.ecovillage.org

Other GEN websites

Each of the seven GEN regions, GEN-International, GEN-Africa, GEN-Europe, GEN-NA, GENOA, CASA and NextGEN — have their own regional website with specific information regarding each region.

genoa.ecovillage.org

GENOA is a network of people, ecovillages and organisations in the region of Oceania & Asia.

genna.ecovillage.org

GENNA - the Ecovillage Network of North America and is active primarily in the United States and Canada.

gen.ecovillage.org

GEN-International is the umbrella organization which represents all of the regional networks and supports the global movement of ecovillages as a whole. Here you can also find news, events, resources and information relevant to GEN on a global level.

gen-europe.org

GEN-Europe is the European ecovillage association promoting social resilience, environmental protection and restoration of nature through the concept of ecovillages as models for sustainable human settlements.

gen-africa.ecovillage.org

GEN-Africa is the African ecovillage association, promoting social

231

resilience, environmental protection and restoration of nature through the concept of ecovillages as models for sustainable human settlements.

casa.ecovillage.org

CASA is the Council of the Americas Sustainable Settlements, which coordinates and strengthens Latin American national networks that promote, educate, investigate and disseminate sustainable lifestyles.

sites.ecovillage.org

GEN Sites is the online community platform of the Global Ecovillage Network. A multitude of features support networking and collaborative project development. It includes news and events from the network as well as a Forum and Marketplace. It also includes a database of information about projects and ecovillages from around the world.

db.ecovillage.org

The GEN Database gives a clean interface to view and manage projects and events in our online community platform. It provides access to the same data that can be accessed through GEN Sites, but without the social features. It focuses on providing a clean and structured experience.

solution.ecovillage.org

We face many challenges in our time. At the same time, there are a great many solutions out there and many people eager to implement them. The Solution Library connects these two. It creates a simple access interface, with clear routes leading users to the information they are searching for. The aim is to make solutions for the transition to sustainability universally accessible.

The solutions library has been established to bring together people and solutions to create a future for humankind and all life. It provides a platform for sharing the solutions that are hidden in the corners of the world, gathering them all in one easy-to-browse website.

What's more, it also provides the ability to share experiences with using the solutions, and members can connect with one another, or with the projects where the solutions are used. In this way, the Solution Library facilitates the global exchange of knowledge and expertise, empowering people everywhere in applying workable solutions. And perhaps the best thing: it's all for free! We warmly invite you to browse, share and connect.

Enjoy!

GEN and Gaia Education: the landscape of collaboration in the fiery urgency of now

Gaia Education was born of the networks of GEN, created over a series of meetings between ecovillage educators and academic and professional backgrounds in a wide range of disciplines. A key achievement of this gifted think-thank was the development of the Ecovillage Design Education (EDE) curriculum, drawing on the experience and expertise of a network of some of the most successful ecovillages and community projects worldwide.

For the last decade Gaia Education has been empowering change-makers with the skills to redesign the human presence in the world. It has successfully supported the delivery of more than 180 programmes in 34 countries over 5 continents, reaching over 5,000 people. These programmes have been offered in tribal and traditional communities, intentional ecovillages, urban slums, universities and training centres.

The courses qualify students of all ages with the appropriate skills and analytical tools to design a society which uses energy and materials with greater efficiency, distributes wealth fairly, and strives to eliminate waste. Students become sustainability designers, taking active roles in transitioning their existing communities, institutions and neighbourhoods to more sustainable patterns of production and consumption, as well as leading more joyful, meaningful and healthy lives. Today Gaia Education has diversified its activities into three learning streams:

- Face-face EDE certified programmes in partnership with over 60 institutions worldwide
- E-learning Design for Sustainability global classrooms in English, Spanish and Portuguese
- Project-based learning activities in the Global South, supporting the implementation of the MDGs and the post-2015 development agenda.

In our multiply connected world we are the first generation that can end poverty and the last generation that can take bold steps to avoid the worst effects of resource depletion and climate change. 2015 marks the consolidation of the Sustainable Development Goals providing a once-in-a-generation opportunity for transformative change and potentially ushering in a new cycle of shared prosperity and a sustainable future for all. 2015 also marks 10 years of Gaia Education and 20 years of GEN — our sister organisation and synergistic partner over the last decade. We take this joint birthday as an opportunity to reinvigorate and strengthen our collaboration in the fiery urgency of now.

LIterature List

Literature

Abouleish, Ibrahim. (2005) . *Sekem: A Sustainable Community in the Egyptian Desert.* Edinburgh. Floris Books

Bang, Jan Martin. (2005) *Ecovillages: A Practical Guide to Sustainable Communities.* Edinburgh: Floris Books.

Barton, H. (ed) (2000a). *Sustainable Communities: The Potential for Eco-Neighbourhoods.* London: Earthscan Publications Ltd.

Bauman, Zygmunt. (2001) *Community: Seeking Safety in an insecure World.* Cambridge.

Bossel, Hartmut. (1999) "Indicators for sustainable development: theory, method, applications. A report to the Balaton Group." IISD, Winnipeg. www.ulb.ac.be/ceese/STAFF/Tom/bossel.pdf

Chatterton, Paul and Alice Cutler. (2008) *The Rocky Road to a Real Transition: The Transition Towns Movement and What it Means for Social Change.* Education Collective Trapese. www.stuffit.org/trapese/

Christian, Diane Leafe. (2003) *Creating a Life together: Practical Tools to Grow Ecovillages and Intentional Communities.* Canada: New Society Publishers.

Dawson, Jonathan. (2006) *Ecovillages: New Frontiers for Sustainability.* Devon: Green Books Ltd.

Dawson, Jonathan, and Helena Norberg-Hodge and Ross Jackson. (2010) *Economic Key: Gaian Economics Living Well within Planetary Limits.* UK: Permanent Publications.

Duhm, Dieter. (2001). *The Sacred Matrix: From the Matrix of Violence to the Matrix of Life. The Foundation for a New Civilization.* Wiesenburg: Meiga Publishing.

EDE (Ecovillage Design Education) (2005): a four-week comprehensive course to the fundamentals of Ecovillage Design for Urban and Rural Settlements. Endorsed by UNITAR- United Nations Institute for Training and Research. Version 3.0: 21.09.05. Director: May East. www.gaiaeducation.org/ http://ecovillage.wikicities.com/wiki/Gaia_ Education 04.04.09

Eurotopia. 1998-2004. Intentional Communities and Ecovillages in Europe. Poppau. Also: www.eurotopia.de

Ergas, C. (2010) "A Model of Sustainable Living: Collective Identity in an

Urban Ecovillage." *Organization & Environment* 23(1):32-54.

Social Key - Beyond You and Me: Inspiration and Wisdom for Building Community Editors: Anja Kosha Joubert and Robin Alfred

Economic Key – Gaian Economics – Living well within planetary limits Editors: Jonathan Dawson, Helena Norberg-Hodge and Ross Jackson

Ecological Key – Designing Ecological Habitats – Creating a Sense of Place Editors: Chris Mare and Max Lindegger

Worldview Key– The Song of the Earth – A Synthesis of the Scientific and Spiritual Worldviews

Garden, M. (2006) "The Eco-Village Movement: Divorced from Reality." *The International Journal of Inclusive Democracy* 2(3):1-5.

Gilman, Robert and Diane Gilman, "Ecovillages and Sustainable Communities: A Report for Gaia Trust," (Gaia Trust, 1991).

Hopkins, R. J. (2010) "Localisation and Resilience at the Local Level: The Case of Transition Town Totnes (Devon, UK)." PhD-thesis, University of Plymouth.

Jackson, Hildur. (1999). *Creating Harmony: Conflict Resolution in Communities.* UK: Permanent

Publications and Gaia Trust.

Jackson, Hildur, and Karen Svensson. (2002) *Ecovillage Living: Restoring the Earth and Her People.* UK: Green Books.

Jackson, J. T. Ross. (2000) *And We ARE Doing It: Building an Ecovillage Future.* San Francisco: Robert D. Reed Publishers.

Jackson, J.T Ross. (1996) *The earth is our habitat : proposal for a support programme for eco-habitats as living examples of Agenda 21 planning* Denmark: Holte, Gaia Trust; Global Eco-Village Network;

Jackson, J. T. Ross. 2012. *Occupy World Street: A Global Roadmap for Radical Economic and Political Reform.* White River Junction VT: Chelsea Green Publishing.

Joss, S. (2011) "Eco-Cities: The Mainstreaming Of Urban Sustainability – Key Characteristics And Driving Factors." *International Journal of Sustainable Development and Planning* 3(6): 268-285.

Joubert, Anja Kosha, and Robin Alfred. (2007) Social Key: Beyond You and Me. UK: Permanent Publications.

Joubert, Anja Kosha. (2010) Die Kraft der Kollektiven Weisheit. Wie wir gemeinsam schaffen, was einer alleine nicht kann. Germany: Kamphausen.

Keepin, William, and Maddy Harland Worldview *Key: The Song of the Earth A Synthesis of the Scientific and Spiritual Worldviews*. UK: Permanent Publications.

Kunze, I. (2012) "Social Innovations for Communal and Ecological Living: Lessons from Sustainability Research and Observations in Intentional Communities", *Communal Societies. Journal of the Communal Studies Association* 32(1): 50-67.

Kunze, Iris and Flor Avelino (2009) "Exploring Ecovillages as alternative fields of sustainability and governance". Presentation at the European Conference on Interpretive Policy Analysis, June 2009, Kassel. Forthcoming publication in: *Critical policy journal*.

Kyvelou, S. (2011) "Exploring a South-European eco-neighbourhood model: planning forms, constraints of implementation and emerging resilience practices." *International Journal of Sustainable Development* 14(1/2):77-94.

Litfin, Karen. 2013. *Ecovillages: Lessons for Sustainable Community*. UK: Polity Press.

Mare, Christopher E., and Max Lindegger. (2011). Ecological Key: Designing Ecological Habitats Creating a Sense of Place. UK: Permanent Publications.

Merrifield, Jeff. (1998) *Damanhur: The Real Dream*. London: Thorsons.

Newhouse, Brian. (2012) *Permaville: How to Design a Permanent Village*. USA.

Schwarz, Walter and Dorothy Schwarz. (1998) *Living Lightly: Travels in Post-Consumer Society*. Oxfordshire: Jon Carpenter Publishing.

Sullivan, W. M. (1994) *The Dawning of Auroville*. Auroville, India: Auroville Press.

Walker, Liz. (2005) *Ecovillage at Ithaca: Pioneering a Sustainable Culture*. Canada: New Society Publishers.

237

TRIARCHY PRESS

Triarchy Press is an independent publisher of new alternative thinking (altThink) about government, organisations and society, and practical ways to apply that thinking. Our authors encourage us to challenge familiar ways of thinking (conThink) and embrace the potential of change.

Our titles cover a wide range of topics including:

Finance, Economics & Money

Money and Sustainability - Bernard Lietaer *et al*

People Money: The promise of regional currencies by Margit Kennedy, Bernard Lietaer and John Rogers

Local Money: What's the point? by John Rogers

Cultural Theory and Clumsy Solutions

Organising and Disorganising by Michael Thompson

Complexity Demystified by Patrick Beautement, Christine Broenner

Shaping the Future

Humanising Healthcare by (Dr.) Margaret Hannah

Dancing at the Edge by Maureen O'Hara and Graham Leicester

Thrivability by Jean Russell

Three Horizons: The Patterning of Hope by Bill Sharpe

Systems Thinking

We have a wealth of books on systems thinking by various authors including Russ Ackoff. Please visit our website and look in the subject area tab.

Mythogeography and Counter Tourism by Crabman...Phil Smith

Society, Somatics, Movement

Embodied Lives: Reflections on the Influence of Suprapto Suryodarmo and Amerta Movement

Attending to Movement: Somatic Perspectives on Living in this World

tp

www.triarchypress.net

About the authors

Kosha Anja Joubert is an international facilitator, trainer, manager and consultant. She has worked extensively in the fields of curriculum development, international collaboration and sustainable development. Kosha grew up in South Africa, and has subsequently lived in intentional communities and researched intercultural communication for the past 25 years. Currently, she lives with her family in Findhorn, Scotland, and serves as President of the Global Ecovillage Network (GEN-International). Kosha is a co-founder of Gaia Education, which develops trainings at the cutting-edge of sustainability, and is a co-author of the internationally applied curriculum of the Ecovillage Design Education. She is especially fascinated by the phenomenon of Collective Wisdom: how can we transform our teams, organisations and societies into systems of cooperation, creativity and innovation. She is currently working on the translation of her book, previously published in German: *The Change Makers Guide to Collective Wisdom*.

Leila Dregger is a graduate agricultural engineer and long-time journalist. She has travelled through all continents to various communities and peace projects to learn about different lifestyle's and to write about them. Her main emphasis is on peace, ecology, community and women. she has worked for the press and radio for 25 years, and is a screenwriter and director for both stage and film. She was the editor of the magazine *The female voice - politics of the heart*. She was press officer of the *house of democracy* in Berlin, the ZEGG in Belzig and Tamera in Portugal, where she mainly lives today. Since 2012, she has been the editor of the GEN-International Newsletters. She teaches constructive journalism for young professionals and students, as well as for journalists working in crisis regions. She is the author of several books.